THE NEW AMERICAN PAINTING

As Shown in Eight European Countries 1958-1959

Organized by the International Program
of The Museum of Modern Art, New York
under the auspices of the International Council at
The Museum of Modern Art, New York

THE MUSEUM OF MODERN ART, NEW YORK

Distributed by Doubleday & Company Inc., Garden City, New York

This catalogue is a reprint of the one which was used for the exhibition in London at the Tate Gallery, February-March, 1959. Color plates and a report of the exhibition's reception abroad have been added.

THE INTERNATIONAL COUNCIL AT THE MUSEUM OF MODERN ART

OFFICERS

Chairman of the Board: August Heckscher, *New York*
President: Mrs Bliss Parkinson, *New York*
Vice-President: Ralph F. Colin, *New York*
Vice-President: John de Menil, *Houston, Texas*
Secretary: Mrs Gilbert W. Chapman, *New York*
Treasurer: Mrs Frederick W. Hilles, *New Haven, Connecticut*
Assistant Treasurer: Mrs Cable Senior, *New York*

HONORARY MEMBERS

The Honourable C. Douglas Dillon, Deputy Under Secretary of State, *Washington*, Senator J. William Fulbright, *Washington*, Dr Will Grohmann, *Berlin*, The Honourable Dag Hammarskjold, Secretary General, The United Nations, Sir Herbert Read, President, The Institute of Contemporary Arts, *London*, Professor Paul J. Sachs, Director Emeritus, The Fogg Art Museum, *Cambridge, Massachusetts*, M. Georges Salles, Former Director, The National Museums of France, *Paris*, Professor Lionello Venturi, *Rome*.

MEMBERS

Larry L. Aldrich, *New York*, Mrs Ernest Angell, *New York*, William Benton, *Southport, Connecticut*, LeRay W. Berdeau, *Palm Beach, Florida*, Robert Woods Bliss, *Washington, D.C.*, Mrs Harry Lynde Bradley★, *Milwaukee*, Mrs Samuel Bronfman, *Montreal*, Shirley C. Burden★, *Beverly Hills, California*, Mrs Gilbert W. Chapman★, *New York*, Ralph F. Colin★, *New York*, Louis G. Cowan★, *New York*, William Willard Crocker, *Burlingame, California*, Mrs Ethel W. de Croisset, *Paris, France*, John de Menil★, *Houston*, Mrs C. Douglas Dillon, *Washington, D.C.*, Allan D. Emil★, *New York*, Julius Fleischmann★, *Cincinnati*, Mrs Walter B. Ford II★, *Grosse Pointe Farms, Michigan*, Mrs Dorothy Hales Gary, *New York*, Mrs Robert D. Graff, *Far Hills, New Jersey*, Mrs Walter A. Haas★, *San Francisco*, Wallace K. Harrison★, *New York*, Mrs Ira Haupt, *New York*, August Heckscher★, *New York*, Mrs Henry J. Heinz II★, *Pittsburgh*, Mrs Frederick W. Hilles★, *New Haven, Connecticut*, Maurice Hirsch★, *Houston*, Mrs Walter Hochschild★, *New York*, Jay Holmes, *New York*, Amory Houghton, *Corning, New York*, Philip C. Johnson★, *New Canaan, Connecticut*, William T. Kemper★, *Kansas City, Missouri*, Mrs William L. Kistler, Jr, *Tulsa*, Mrs Phyllis B. Lambert★, *New York*, Mrs Fernand Leval★, *New York*, Mrs H. Gates Lloyd★, *Washington, D.C.*, James H. Lockhart, Jr, *Geneseo, New York*, Stanley Marcus★, *Dallas*, Mrs Samuel A. Marx★, *Chicago*, Porter A. McCray★, *New York*, Mrs Gertrud A. Mellon★, *Greenwich, Connecticut*, Mrs G. Macculloch Miller, *New York*, Mr Jan Mitchell, *New York*, Henry Allen Moe★, *New York*, John S. Newberry, *New York*, Carleton H. Palmer, *New York*, Mrs Bliss Parkinson★, *New York*, Duncan Phillips,

ITINERARY OF THE NEW AMERICAN PAINTING

4

FOREWORD

The International Program of the Museum of Modern Art was established in 1952. Since then it has sent to all parts of the world fifty exhibitions of painting and sculpture, prints, architecture and design, photography and the film. This is the first full-scale exhibition prepared for circulation outside the United States which we have been able to show in the Museum itself.

The New American Painting was organized at the request of European institutions for a show devoted specifically to Abstract Expressionism in America. Most of the artists have been shown in the Museum, but even in New York we have not until now undertaken so comprehensive a survey. Although works by many of them were previously known in Europe, often from exhibitions circulated by the International Program, the few quotations on pages 7-14 give only a slight idea of Europe's present interest in American art, stimulated by this exhibition. Concrete evidence may be found in the increasing number of purchases for public and private collections in Europe.

We must express our gratitude to many: to those individuals and organizations in the United States and Europe whose interest and assistance brought the exhibition into being; to the institutions where it was shown; to our generous and patient lenders; to the United States Lines, which transported the paintings to and from Europe without charge.

We are grateful to the International Council at the Museum of Modern Art for enabling the International Program to carry out this project, and we are indebted to the staff of the Program and particularly to its Director, Porter A. McCray, for the meticulous care with which the exhibition has been organized and presented in each of the eight European countries to which it has travelled. First and last, *The New American Painting* demonstrates the knowledge and experience of its director, Dorothy C. Miller. Her insight and that of Alfred H. Barr, Jr., who provided the introduction to this catalogue, are evident in many of the exhibitions at the Museum and in the acquisition of works of art for the Museum Collection.

For us, our reward is the pleasure of knowing that this exhibition and those before it have won for American art widespread recognition and acclaim abroad.

RENE D'HARNONCOURT
Director
The Museum of Modern Art

ACKNOWLEDGMENT

On behalf of the International Program of the Museum of Modern Art, I wish to express my gratitude to the artists who have taken part in the exhibition and to the lenders whose names are listed below. The exhibition was made possible through the generosity of the collectors, museums and dealers who graciously permitted their paintings to travel for over a year. Their understanding of the purposes of the exhibition and their readiness to help overcome the difficulties of assembling it deserve the greatest appreciation. I am indebted for expert assistance in organizing the exhibition to Frank O'Hara of the International Program and in preparing the catalogue to Miss Helen Franc. The dealers representing artists in the exhibition have been most helpful in supplying information and photographs. Grateful acknowledgment is made also to the photographers who supplied portraits of the artists, and to the various publications from which statements by the artists and others have been quoted.

DOROTHY C. MILLER
Director of the Exhibition

LENDERS TO THE EXHIBITION

Richard Brown Baker, *New York*, Mr and Mrs Walter Bareiss, *Greenwich, Connecticut*, Dr and Mrs Edgar Berman, *Baltimore*, Mr and Mrs Donald M. Blinken, *New York*, Mr and Mrs William A. M. Burden, *New York*, Mr and Mrs William Calfee, *Washington, D.C.*, Mrs Leo Castelli, *New York*, John M. Cuddihy, *New York*, Adolph Gottlieb, *New York*, Mr and Mrs Clement Greenberg, *New York*, Mr and Mrs I. Donald Grossman, *New York*, Mr and Mrs Ben Heller, *New York*, Philip C. Johnson, *New Canaan, Connecticut*, Boris and Sophie Leavitt, *Lana Lobell, Hanover, Pennsylvania*, Mrs H. Gates Lloyd, *Haverford, Pennsylvania*, Mr and Mrs Patrick B. McGinnis, *Boston*, Mr and Mrs Roy R. Neuberger, *New York*, Mr and Mrs Albert Newman, *Chicago*, Mrs Bliss Parkinson, *New York*, Mrs Betty Parsons, *New York*, Mr and Mrs George Poindexter, *New York*, E. J. Power, *London*, Mr and Mrs Paul Rankine, *Bethesda, Maryland*, Mrs John D. Rockefeller III, *New York*, Governor Nelson A. Rockefeller, *New York*, Mrs Sherman J. Sexton, *Chicago*, Mr and Mrs Thomas Sills, *New York*, Tom Slick, *San Antonio, Texas*, Mr and Mrs Anthony Smith, *South Orange, New Jersey*, Dr and Mrs Frank Stanton, *New York*, Mr and Mrs John Stephan, *Greenwich, Connecticut*, Mr and Mrs Guy A. Weill, *Scarsdale, New York*.

André Emmerich Gallery, *New York*, Martha Jackson Gallery, *New York*, Sidney Janis Gallery, *New York*, Betty Parsons Gallery, *New York*, Stable Gallery, *New York*.

The Minneapolis Institute of Arts, The Philadelphia Museum of Art, The Museum of Modern Art, *New York*.

AS THE CRITICS SAW IT

In the space of a year, *The New American Painting* was seen in eight cities in eight countries. In each city the exhibition was held in the major institution associated with modern art and a catalogue similar to this was issued in the language of the country. It is not hard to imagine the quantity of journalism generated, nor the difficulty of assessing the response. It is true to say that the paintings created a sensation: whether enthusiastically, hesitantly, in the form of back-handed compliments, or of real hostility, it was acknowledged that in America a totally 'new' – a unique and indigenous – kind of painting has appeared, one whose influence can be clearly seen in works of artists in Europe as well as in many other parts of the world. The quotations are necessarily brief. Elisions are not indicated, but we have tried not to distort any writer's main intent.

PORTER MCCRAY

BASEL, SWITZERLAND
Kunsthalle
19 April – 26 May 1958

The great reach of American painting becomes apparent when it not only comprises segments of reality dipped into vivid color by Hartigan, but also the severity of Barnett Newman, although the main influence lies in the direction of *Tachisme*. European influences are caught in the occasional appearance of painterly effects, particularly in absorbing surrealist motifs. Of Kandinsky, who means so much to European abstract painting, there is strikingly little, which is interesting because of the central position that the realization of spatial concept takes up in American painting. This in particular is its decisive character: the direct translation of unlimited space into the gesture of

painting itself, whether into expanding form or the continual overflow and inter-mingling of forms; it is creation which tries for the domination of space. This impelling urge toward utter freedom and uninhibited statement frees this style of painting of all symbolic sign language and allows it to reach the most spontaneous manifestation of emotion.

HELMI GASSER, *Neue Zürcher Zeitung*, Zurich, May 23, 1958

It is not new. It is not painting. It is not American. There is no deep necessity, no inner torment, not even a serious formal research. Not one of these painters goes against the current. Not one of them is anti-conformist. There is no spiritual flight.

LEONARDO BORGESE, *Corriere della Sera*, Milan, June 8, 1958

One should not forget that while on the Atlantic coast there was close contact with Europe, on the Pacific, in San Francisco, there were more diverse graftings: the totem poles of the Indians and the Mexicans' intricate baroque, the symbolic and ancient scripts of China and Japan. Such important and stimulating facts could not remain dormant in soil so rich. And the difficulties encountered by this new generation of painters in trying to pierce the indifference of the American public, the necessity of surviving as individuals without being crushed by the conformism of industrialized life, have added that charge of violence and of personal fury which each of these paintings conveys. It is like witnessing a shipwreck and their fight for survival.

The rapidity and vigor of the results are astonishing. To be objective, I must say that American art derives from European art and is still sensitive to its cultural echoes, but nevertheless its character is so well defined, the images are so abundant and so per-meated by the fantasy and motivations of Americans ideals, that one must admit it has by now the look of independence, decisively recognizable.

I feel that this process is taking place among these Americans with unexpected tender-ness and lightness of touch, with a feeling of happiness, in spite of past anxieties. This

8

recalls Matisse, and, less directly, Impressionism. Their creative talent is more free because they are not bound to traditions, to deep-rooted cultures, as our artists are. Therefore the American artists succeed in reaching a greater freedom, with results more pleasant, vibrant, and cheerful. We had been told that they were wild: we find instead a festive pictorial quality without dramatic shocks; including Pollock, who plunged deepest into the intricate web of pictorial experiments.

MARCO VALSECCHI, *Il Giorno*, Milan, June 10, 1958

MADRID, SPAIN
Museo Nacional de Arte Contemporáneo
16 July – 10 August 1958

I had resigned myself to not seeing the exhibition. But others did not resign themselves, and thus in rapid, improvised, and exhausting days, it was possible to move eighty-one canvases, packed in more than forty enormous cases, from Milan to Madrid. To judge the size of the transoceanic guests, a detail will suffice: to bring into the Museum two of the canvases, one by Jackson Pollock and one by Grace Hartigan, required sawing the upper part of the metal entrance door of the building the night before the inauguration.

Upon entering the room, a strange sensation like that of magnetic tension surrounds you, as though the expression concentrated in the canvases would spring from them. They are other myths, other gods, other ideas, different from those prevailing in Europe at present, and from that grayish and textured Parisian fog which also in this country of light and color today masks the polychromatic traditions.

Each picture is a confession, an intimate chat with the Divinity, accepting or denying the exterior world but always faithful to the more profound identity of conscience. The present painting is a mystery to many who wish to understand its significance without entering into its state, thereby committing an error as profound as he who wishes to attain the Moradas of Teresa de Avila by means of intelligence and not by means of Grace.

MERCEDES MOLLEDA, *Revista*, Barcelona, August 30, 1958

In view of the large number of great talents, one can speak of an American School; for the first time in the history of art, personalities are emerging that are not influenced by Europe, but, on the contrary, influence Europe, including Paris. For nearly ten years Pollock has exerted his influence on the *avant-garde* of all countries. The appearance of his paintings in Paris and in Venice was a sensation; and since the young Sam Francis lives in Paris, he too is in the center of international interest. The unshakable fortress of the French School is shaken.

Pollock was a genius, but by European standards, one can easily count half of the other sixteen to be exceptional talents. They are painters without regard for the ready-made world. What they paint is real; it is the spectator himself who must have a certain amount of imagination in order to comprehend. Without an actual consciousness of the universe this is not possible. Here, there is no comfort, but a struggle with the elements, with society, with fate. It is like the American novel; something happens, and what happens is disquieting and at the same time pregnant with the future.

Robert Motherwell and Franz Kline stand apart from the rest. They paint gigantic symbols on the wall and call their proclamations *Elegy for the Spanish Republic XXXV* or *Accent Grave*. The paintings are hypotheses of what could come; but poems by Ezra Pound or the Spaniard Guillén are exactly as hypothetical if one starts with the limitations of one's own imagination. What makes these painters artists is the advance into a world which is not prefabricated, but for that reason is also not boarded up; on the contrary, it is so vast that one hardly dares to enter it. What is emphasized here? An event that starts like a poem by Ezra Pound and ends with a statute for the investigation of the space of the universe. Greece is not a European suburb any more.

They all use vast dimensions, not from megalomania, but because one cannot say these things in miniature. Klee was able to do just that; his world was not smaller because of it; he was a monk and wrote the psalter of our saeculum. Americans are world travelers and conquerors. They possess an enormous daring. One proves oneself in the doing, in the performance, in the act of creation. In the United States one speaks of Action

Painting. We speak of Abstract Expressionism. This difference characterizes America as well as Europe. We cannot forget, we distill the conceptions of long experience instead of creating new ones. In any case, these young Americans stand beyond heritage and psychology, nearly beyond good and evil. In Europe we are a little bit afraid, confronted by such a lack of prejudice. Could it be that we are already in a state of defense?

WILL GROHMANN, *Der Tagesspiegel*, Berlin, September 7, 1958

AMSTERDAM, NETHERLANDS
Stedelijk Museum
17 October – 24 November 1958

Pollock must be given credit for creating, by colors and the movement of line, a dynamism which fascinates the eye. One feels that he has painted in a kind of ecstasy, supported, however, by authentic skill and by a highly developed gift as a colorist. Thus was his work created; a 'map' of modern life, a map in which areas of chaos are charted. Pictures consisting of angry, confused lines that are gradually acquiring order, the latter eloquently expressed by color. Consequently, the tension in Pollock's paintings contains an element of relaxation.

De Kooning's work is aggressive, filled with wrath and sometimes with repulsion. But it has dynamism and originality; his color as well, which sometimes makes startling contrasts. In this art, conflicts are expressed with a hardness and a temerity which involuntarily remind us of the hard-boiled mentality of modern American literature. Tomlin's work is characterized by a dynamic kind of calligraphy and is therefore an example of the influence of Asian art, which is indeed considerable in America. Franz Kline paints angrily gesticulating signals suggesting danger, hostile barriers, and heads of prehistoric insects.

No matter how subjective their work may be, it has a communicative power because they live under the spell of their time, which is also our time, and because the projection of their personal tensions represents, to some extent, a projection of the spirit of our time, experienced by all of us.

UNSIGNED, *Nieuw Rotterdamse Courant*, Rotterdam, November 15, 1958

BRUSSELS, BELGIUM
Palais des Beaux-Arts
6 December 1958 – 4 January 1959

Primarily, it offers that climate of unconstraint which never fails to strike anyone traveling to the United States for the first time, and of which those of us who strolled this summer through the American Pavillion at the Brussels Fair could form some idea. For us, an avant-garde exhibition still retains a certain quality of provocation and unfailingly arouses a reaction from those who, without any justification one must add, see in it some sort of threat to traditional forms of expression. Two points to be remarked on: the feeling of sincerity produced by the work as a whole, and the intuitive sense generated in the spectator of an absence of gratuitousness.

R.M.T., *La Derniere Heure*, Brussels, December 7, 1958

One examines with consternation ink spots measuring two yards by two and a half; graffiti enlarged ten-thousand times, where a crayon stroke becomes as thick as a rafter; soft rectangles, formless scribblings, childish collections of signs; enough to make our own abstract painters blush for shame, exposed henceforth to the most humiliating comparisons.

UNSIGNED, Le Phare, Brussels, December 14, 1958

It is not only a question of bringing to the public's attention a few American names to slip in next to the 'Parisians', but – more profoundly – of coming to an interesting and opportune awareness of the 'modern adventure' in painting, thanks to the remarkable forms it is taking on the other side of the Atlantic. The seventeen painters chosen clearly define the amplitude of their experiments, from Barnett Newman's concise stripes, Rothko's simple contrasts and the thick black lines of Franz Kline to Guston's semi-impressionist pink flickerings, Brooks' brilliant nests of color, and Sam Francis' rain of petals. We grasp the pleasure that Motherwell, for instance, or Tworkov takes in projecting himself into the formless; Grace Hartigan in producing street scenes of brilliant and clashing patches of color that recall the Fauves; Tomlin in marking out geometrical vibrations that are almost elemental signs. Baziotes, easily the most agreeable member of the group with his rather fragile mauves and greens, stands apart in his lack of frenzy. The two most feverish, and by the same token the most typical, are Willem de Kooning, with his grinning, flayed women, and the touching Gorky. We are dealing with a kind of painting that seems to refuse any frame, any imprisonment; which no longer takes anything into consideration. And which will have the greater difficulties growing old.

All of which emphasizes to an extreme degree the originality of the American scene – or more exactly, of the New York milieu. And yet this show enforces certain analogies. The roots of this art are European, and are called Fauvism, German Expressionism, Klee, Picasso, sometimes Matisse or André Masson's inspired Surrealism. In Europe we have returned by more or less brutal stops and starts to the notion of the 'object' and to the privileges of the *painting* treated as such; in the United States, ingenuous even in their surrealist revolt against the oppression of a mechanistic civilization and its utilitarian nonsense, men have discovered the facility and the strangeness of the very act of painting. There had to be this somewhat blind generosity to which Pollock bears witness to give to this anxiety its whole meaning. Thus develops a difficult and tentative dialogue, which constitutes the value of this century's painting.

ANDRE CHASTEL, *Le Monde*, Paris, January 17, 1959

Why do they think they are painters? We would end up by being, I won't say convinced – for the only greatness here is in the size of the canvases – but disarmed if we did not deplore the terrible danger which the publicity given to such examples offers, as well as the imprudence of the combined national museums in offering official support all too generously to such contagious heresies.

CLAUDE ROGER-MARX, *Le Figaro Littéraire*, Paris, January 19, 1959

Once inside the gallery you can't slide politely past this lot of pictures. If our aesthetic reactions are not numb, scenes of enthusiasm or distress, dancing or denunciation are to be expected at the Tate. During my visit the public was quiet, though I have never seen so many young gallery-goers sitting down in a silent daze.

FREDERICK LAWS, *The Manchester Guardian*, Manchester, February 27, 1959

LONDON, ENGLAND
Tate Gallery
24 February – 23 March 1959

13

What cannot fail to strike any visitor, and strike him forcibly whether he is naturally inclined for or against this development of modern art, is an impression of size; of size, moreover, not merely in an inflatory sense, but as a natural assumption of scale which seems for once to fill, in the most acceptable manner, the Edwardian stateliness of the Tate's towering rooms. The paintings fulfill the demand of the galleries' dimensions, which are not proportioned for individual comfort or domestic relaxation, but for the expansive scale of the social occasion. Though the suggestion may not be readily acceptable in some quarters, it still seems worth remarking that paintings which can function in this manner appear eminently suitable for the public and social role which is so desperately looked for from the art of the present time, a role which can combine the so-called 'environmental' demands of architecture with the qualities of a personal statement. It must, however, be admitted that American painting has perhaps only unconsciously begun to satisfy the former requirement, its conscious pursuit being of the latter. But here again the quality of adventure, of individual striving, of hammering out modes of expression with a pioneering sense of independence, lends these personal utterances a forceful, easily communicable, vitality.

FROM OUR ART CRITIC, *The Times*, London, February 4, 1959

This is not art – it's a joke in bad taste: *Save me from the great string spider webs.*

HEADLINES IN *Reynolds News*, London, March 1, 1959

However often we may have heard of the size, the assurance, the headlong heedless momentum which characterize them all, we are still bowled over by these qualities when we are, as it were, physically involved in them. For involved we are, as if by some vast upheaval, not of Nature, but of our notion of human potentialities. When paintings of this sort were first shown at the Tate, in 1956, I made the error, as it now seems to me, of judging them according to the canons of traditional aesthetics. They do not in reality, relate to these aesthetics at all; or, if they do, it is as a result of what Mr Alfred Barr calls 'an intuitive struggle for order'.

JOHN RUSSELL, *Sunday Times*, London, March 8, 1959

INTRODUCTION

'We are now committed to an unqualified act, not illustrating outworn myths or contemporary alibis. One must accept total responsibility for what he executes.'

CLYFFORD STILL 1952

'Voyaging into the night, one knows not where, on an unknown vessel, an absolute struggle with the elements of the real.'

ROBERT MOTHERWELL

'There is no more forthright a declaration, and no shorter a path to man's richness, nakedness and poverty than the painting he does. Nothing can be hidden on its surface – the least private as well as the most personal of worlds.'

JAMES BROOKS 1956

'Art never seems to make me peaceful or pure . . . I do not think . . . of art as a situation of comfort.'

WILLEM DE KOONING 1951

'The need is for felt experience – intense, immoderate, direct, subtle, unified, warm, vivid, rhythmic.'

ROBERT MOTHERWELL 1951

'Subject is crucial and only that subject matter is crucial which is tragic and timeless.'

MARK ROTHKO

'What happens on the canvas is unpredictable and surprising to me . . . As I work, or when the painting is finished, the subject reveals itself.'

WILLIAM BAZIOTES 1952

'Usually I am on a work for a long stretch, until a moment arrives when the air of the arbitrary vanishes and the paint falls into positions that feel destined . . . To paint is a possessing rather than a picturing.'

PHILIP GUSTON 1956

'The function of the artist is to make actual the spiritual so that it is there to be possessed.'

ROBERT MOTHERWELL

Of the seventeen painters in this exhibition, none speaks for the others any more than he paints for the others. In principle their individualism is as uncompromising as that of the religion of Kierkegaard whom they honour. For them, John Donne to the contrary, each man is an island.

Though a painter's words about his art are not always to be taken at face value, the quotations preceding this preface – like the statements printed further on – suggest that these artists share certain strong convictions. Many feel that their painting is a stubborn, difficult, even desperate effort to discover the 'self' or 'reality', an effort to which the whole personality should be recklessly committed: *I paint, therefore I am.* Confronting a blank canvas they attempt 'to grasp authentic being by action, decision, a leap of faith', to use Karl Jaspers' Existentialist phrase.

Indeed one often hears Existentialist echoes in their words, but their 'anxiety', their 'commitment', their 'dreadful freedom' concern their work primarily. They defiantly reject the conventional values of the society which surrounds them, but they are not politically *engagés* even though their paintings have been praised and condemned as symbolic demonstrations of freedom in a world in which freedom connotes a political attitude.

In recent years, some of the painters have been impressed by the Japanese Zen philosophy with its transcendental humour and its exploration of the self through intuition. Yet, though Existentialism and Zen have afforded some encouragement and sanction to the artists, their art itself has been affected only sporadically by these philosophies (by contrast with that of the older painter, Mark Tobey, whose abstract painting has been deeply and directly influenced by Tao and Zen).

Surrealism, both philosophically and technically, had a more direct effect upon the painting of the group. Particularly in the early days of the movement, during the war, several painters were influenced by André Breton's programme of 'pure psychic automatism . . . in the absence of all control exercised by reason and outside of all aesthetic and moral preoccupation'. Automatism was, and still is, widely used as a technique but rarely without some control or subsequent revision. And from the first Breton's dependence upon Freudian and Marxian sanctions seemed less relevant than Jung's concern with myth and archaic symbol.

The artists in the exhibition comprise the central core as well as the major marginal talent in the movement now generally called 'Abstract Expressionism' or, less commonly, 'Action Painting'. Both terms were considered as titles for this exhibition.

Abstract Expressionism, a phrase used ephemerally in Berlin in 1919, was re-invented (by the writer) about 1929 to designate Kandinsky's early abstractions that in certain ways do anticipate the American movement – to which the term was first applied in 1946. However, almost to a man, the painters in this show deny that their work is 'abstract', at least in any pure, programmatic sense; and they rightly reject any significant association with German Expressionism, a movement recently much exhibited in America.

Action Painting, a phrase proposed in preference to Abstract Expressionism by the poet-critic, Harold Rosenberg, in an important article published in 1952 (see below*), now seems to overemphasize the physical act of painting. Anyway, these artists dislike labels and shun the words 'movement' and 'school'.

* Harold Rosenberg, 'American Action Painters', *Art News*, Vol. 51, December 1952.

16

The briefest glance around the exhibition reveals a striking variety among the paintings. How could canvases differ more in form than do Kline's broad, slashing blacks from Rothko's dissonant mists, or Pollock's Dionysiac *perpetuum mobile* from Newman's single, obsessive, vertical line? What then unites these paintings?

Size

First, their size. Painted at arm's length, with large gestures, they challenge both the painter and the observer. They envelop the eye, they seem immanent. They are often as big as mural paintings, but their scale as well as their lack of illusionistic depth are only coincidentally related to architectural decoration. Their flatness is, rather, a consequence of the artist's concern with the actual painting process as his prime instrument of expression, a concern which also tends to eliminate imitative suggestion of the forms, textures, colours and spaces of the real world, since these might compete with the primary reality of paint on canvas.

why not a struggle for disorder

As a consequence, rather than by intent, most of the paintings seem abstract. Yet they are never formalistic or non-objective in spirit. Nor is there (in theory) any preoccupation with the traditional aesthetics of 'plastic values', composition, quality of line, beauty of surface, harmony of colour. When these occur in the paintings – and they often do – it is the result of a struggle for order almost as intuitive as the initial chaos with which the paintings begin.

Despite the high degree of abstraction, the painters insist that they are deeply involved with subject matter or content. The content, however, is never explicit or obvious even when recognizable forms emerge, as in certain paintings by de Kooning, Baziotes, and Gottlieb. Rarely do any conscious associations explain the emotions of fear, gaiety, anger, violence, or tranquillity which these paintings transmit or suggest.

In short these painters, as a matter of principle, do nothing deliberately in their work to make 'communication' easy. Yet in spite of their intransigence, their following increases, largely because the paintings themselves have a sensuous, emotional, aesthetic and at times almost mystical power which works and can be overwhelming.

The movement began some fifteen years ago in wartime New York. American painting in the early 1940's was bewilderingly varied and without dominant direction. The 'old masters' such as John Marin, Edward Hopper, Max Weber, Stuart Davis, were more than holding their own. The bumptious Mid-Western regionalism of the 1930's, though still noisy, was dying along with its political analogue, 'America First' isolationism. Most of the artists who during the decade of the Great Depression had been naïvely attracted by Communism had grown disillusioned both with the machinations of the party and with Socialist Realism. There were romantic realists who looked back nostalgically to the early nineteenth century, and 'magic realists', and painters of the social

17

scene such as the admirable Ben Shahn. The young Boston expressionists Hyman Bloom and Jack Levine had considerable success in New York, while from the Pacific coast came the visionary art of Mark Tobey and Morris Graves, reflecting Oriental influence in spirit and technique. There was also a lively interest in modern primitives, but no one discovered an American *douanier* Rousseau.

Late in the artistically reactionary 1930's, the American Abstract Artists group had stood firm along with their allies, *Abstraction-Création* in Paris and Unit One in England. Working principally in rather dry cubist or non-objective styles, they did not seem much affected by the arrival in the United States of Léger, Mondrian and several Bauhaus masters. Quite other young painters, not yet identified as a group, were however strongly influenced by the surrealist refugees from the war, notably Max Ernst, André Masson, Marcel Duchamp (who had been the leader of New York Dadaism during World War I), the poet André Breton, and the young Chilean-Parisian painter Matta Echaurren. Equally important was the influence of the former surrealist associates, Picasso, Miró and Arp, who had stayed in Europe.

Chief among the supporters of the surrealist group in New York was Peggy Guggenheim whose gallery, 'Art of This Century', opened in the autumn of 1942 and served as the principal centre of the *avant-garde* in American painting until the founder returned to Europe in 1947. Her brilliant pioneering was then carried on by the new galleries of Betty Parsons, Charles Egan and Sam Kootz. 'Art of This Century' gave one-man shows to Motherwell, Baziotes, Rothko and Still, and no less than four to Jackson Pollock. Arshile Gorky, the most important early master of the movement, showed at another (and prior) surrealist centre, the Julien Levy Gallery, with the poetic blessing of Breton.

The work of certain older American painters, notably Ryder, Marin and Dove, interested some of the artists, and for a time Rothko, Pollock, Gottlieb and Still were influenced by the symbolic imagery of primitive art, especially of the American northwest coast. All during this early period and afterwards, Hans Hofmann, a Parisian-trained German of Picasso's generation, taught the young inspiringly and became their *doyen* colleague, though with little obvious effect on the leaders.

Before 1950 most of the artists in this show had hit their stride. And they had won general, though usually reluctant, recognition as the flourishing vanguard of American painting, thanks to the courageous dealers just mentioned, enthusiastic critics such as Clement Greenberg, a handful of editors, teachers, collectors, and museum officials, and above all to their own extraordinary energy, talent, and fortitude.

They were not, however, a compact phalanx. Gorky had been a quite well-known but rather derivative painter for fifteen years before he found himself about 1943. Pollock and Baziotes, both born in 1912, worked in obscurity until 1942–3, when they emerged along with the youthful and articulate Motherwell. Pollock exhibited his first highly abstract pictures about 1945 and invented his 'drip' technique in 1947. [Exhibitions early in 1959 confirmed that Pollock had painted abstract expressionist paintings as early as 1937; and that Hofmann was using a drip technique as early as 1940.] By 1947, Rothko and Still, working some of the time in California, were developing their characteristic styles, Gottlieb was turning away from his 'pictographic' forms, and Stamos, twenty years younger than they, had had his first show. In 1948, de Kooning, then forty-four, publicly entered the movement and quickly became a major figure; Tomlin was nearly fifty. Kline, Newman, Brooks and Guston, all mature painters, also transformed their art, Guston after having relinquished a brilliant success in a more realistic style. Since 1950, hundreds upon hundreds of American artists have turned to 'abstract expressionism', some of them, like Tworkov, in mid-career, others like Hartigan and Francis while they were still students. Sam Francis is unique as the only expatriate in the show and the only painter whose reputation was made without benefit of New York, having moved directly to Paris from San Francisco where Still and Rothko had been honoured and influential teachers. Sculptors related to, and sometimes closely allied with, the painters' movement should be mentioned, notably Herbert Ferber, David Hare, Ibram Lassaw, Seymour Lipton, Theodore Roszak and David Smith.

The movement, after several tentative early years, has flourished in its maturity since about 1948, roughly the starting point of this show. Naturally, because of its dominance, it has aroused much resistance in the United States among other artists and the public, but it has excited widespread interest and even influenced the painting of some of its most stubborn adversaries. Others are staunchly resisting what has inevitably become fashionable. There will be reactions and counter-revolutions – and some are already evident. Fortunately, the undogmatic variety and flexibility inherent in the movement permits divergence even among the leaders; a few years ago, for instance, both Pollock and de Kooning painted a number of pictures with recognizable figures, to the dismay of some of their followers who had been inclined to make an orthodoxy of abstraction.

For over a dozen years now, works by some of these artists have been shown abroad, first in Europe, then in Latin America and the Orient. They have met with controversy but also with enthusiasm, thanks in part to artists working along similar lines, and to other champions.

To have written a few words of introduction to this exhibition is an honour for an American who has watched with deep excitement and pride the development of the artists here represented, their long struggle – with themselves even more than with the public – and their present triumph.

March, 1958

ALFRED H. BARR, JR

Photograph by Maurice Berezov

WILLIAM BAZIOTES

I cannot evolve any concrete theory about painting. What happens on the canvas is unpredictable and surprising to me. But I am able to speak of certain things that have occurred up to now in the course of my painting.

Today it's possible to paint one canvas with the calmness of an ancient Greek, and the next with the anxiety of a Van Gogh. Either of these emotions, and any in between, is valid to me.

There is no particular system I follow when I begin painting. Each painting has its own way of evolving. One may start with a few color areas on the canvas; another with a myriad of lines; and perhaps another with a profusion of colors.

Each beginning suggests something. Once I sense the suggestion, I begin to paint intuitively. The suggestion then becomes a phantom that must be caught and made real. As I work, or when the painting is finished, the subject reveals itself.

As for the subject matter in my painting, when I am observing something that may be the theme for a painting, it is very often an incidental thing in the background, elusive and unclear, that really stirred me, rather than the thing before me.

I work on many canvases at once. In the morning I line them up against the wall of my studio. Some speak; some do not. They are my mirrors. They tell me what I am like at the moment.

From a statement by the artist in Possibilities, *I, Winter 1947–8 ('Problems of Contemporary Art', No.4, copyright Wittenborn Inc.)*

William Baziotes *Dwarf*, 1947. Oil on canvas 42 × 36⅛ in. Lent by The Museum of Modern Art, New York (A. Conger Goodyear Fund)

William Baziotes *Primeval Landscape*, 1953. Oil on canvas 60 × 72 in.
Lent by the Philadelphia Museum of Art, Philadelphia (Samuel S. Fleisher Art Memorial)

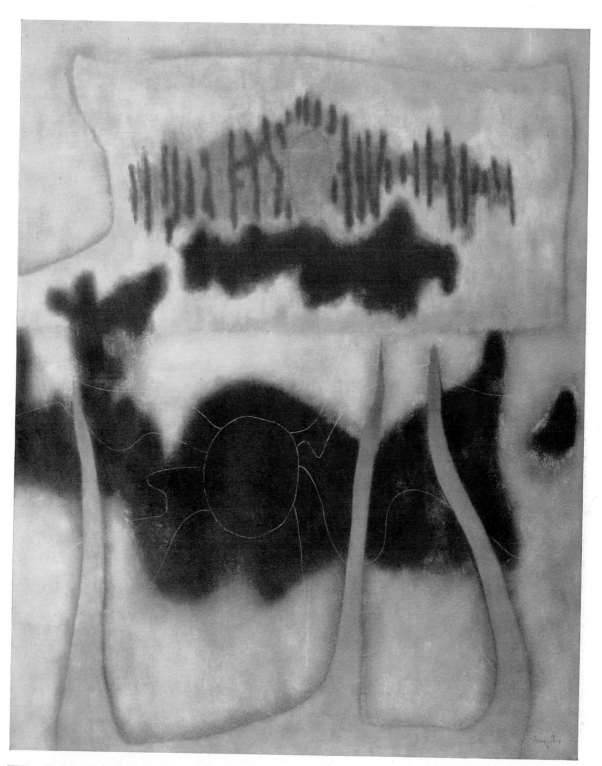

William Baziotes *Pompeii*, 1956. Oil on canvas 60 × 48 ln.
Lent by the Museum of Modern Art, New York (Mrs Louise Smith Fund)

JAMES BROOKS

The painting surface has always been the rendezvous of what the painter knows with the unknown, which appears on it for the first time. An engrossment in the process of changing formal relations is the painter's method of relieving his self-consciousness as he approaches the mystery he hopes for. Any conscious involvement (even thinking of a battle or standing before a still life) is good if it permits the unknown to enter the painting almost unnoticed. Then the painter must hold this strange thing, and sometimes he can, for his whole life has been a preparation for recognizing and resolving it.

Statement by the artist in exhibition catalogue, The New Decade: 35 American Painters and Sculptors, *Whitney Museum of American Art, New York,* 1955.

There is no more forthright a declaration, and no shorter path to man's richness, nakedness and poverty than the painting he does. Nothing can be hidden on its flat surface – the least private as well as the most personal of worlds.

From a statement by the artist in exhibition catalogue, 12 Americans, *The Museum of Modern Art, New York,* 1956.

My work consists almost entirely of curved areas – which suggest natural growth as opposed to the man-made straight lines, angular or rectangular forms. But I do not look at natural growth or forms more often than I look at man-made things, and it never occurs to me in painting that I am taking either from nature or manufacture; everything pools into one source, I suppose, and is unconsciously drawn in . . .

The gestures of the shapes in my paintings are probably taken more from human gestures than from dumb nature. This, though, is only conjecture on my part . . . I know that a painting is not just a complex of the painting elements that exist for the sake of an articulate structure; there is always something that this adds up to which contains the real meaning of the work.

From an unpublished letter to John I. H. Baur, Curator, Whitney Museum of American Art, New York, in reply to questionnaire on the role of nature in abstract art, 1957.

James Brooks *Qualm*, 1954. Oil on canvas 61 × 57⅛ in. Lent by The Museum of Modern Art, New York
(Gift of Mrs Bliss Parkinson)

James Brooks *Jackson*, 1956. Oil on canvas 66¾ × 69¾ in. Lent by Nelson A. Rockefeller, New York

James Brooks *Karrig*, 1956. Oil on canvas 79⅛ × 73½ in. Lent by Stable Gallery, New York

SAM FRANCIS

What we want is to make something that fills
utterly the sight and can't be used to make life
only bearable; if the painting till now was a way
of making bearable the sight of the unbearable,
the visible sumptuous, then let's now strip
away . . . all that.

These paintings lie under the cloud that
soared over the inlaid sea.

Do you still lie dreaming under that huge
canvas? Complete vision abandons the three-
times-divided soul and its vapours; it is the
cloud come over the inlaid sea. You can't inter-
pret the dream of the canvas for this dream is at
the end of the hunt on the heavenly mountain –
where nothing remains but the phoenix caught
in the midst of lovely blueness . . .

Statement by the artist in an unpublished letter (1957)

Sam Francis *Big Red*, 1953.
Oil on canvas 119 × 76 in.
Lent by The Museum of Modern
Art, New York (Gift of
Mr and Mrs David Rockefeller)

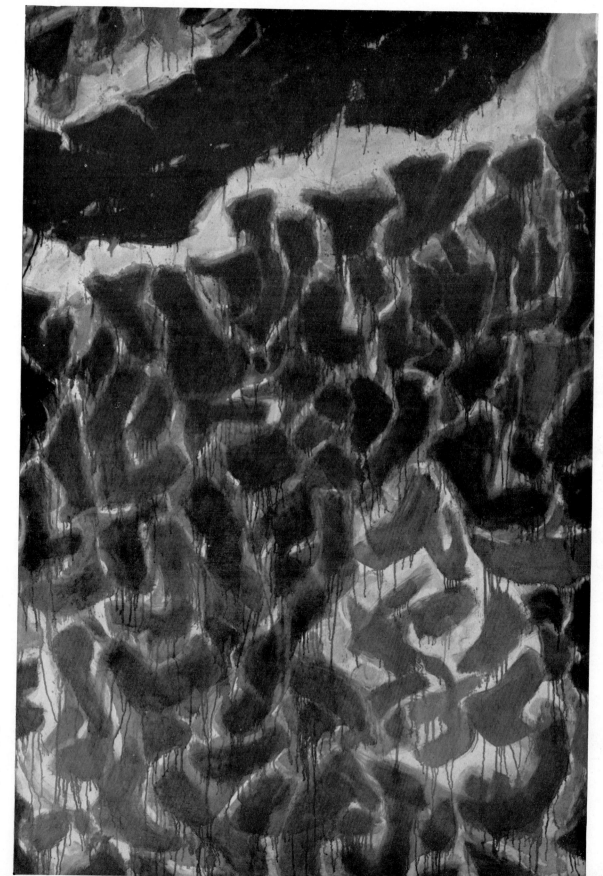

Sam Francis *Black in Red*,
1953, Oil on canvas
77 × 51¼ in. Lent by
The Museum of
Modern Art, New York
(Blanchette Rockefeller
Fund)

Sam Francis
Blue and Black, 1954.
Oil on canvas 77 × 51½ in
Lent by E. J. Power,
London

Photograph by Gjon Mili

ARSHILE GORKY

. . . I say that the eye is not *open* when it is limited to the passive role of a mirror – even if the water of that mirror offers some interesting peculiarities: especially limpid, or sparkling, or boiling, or faceted – that eye impresses me as no less dead than the eye of a slaughtered steer if it has only the capacity to *reflect* – what if it re-flects the object in one or in many aspects, in repose or in motion, in waking or in dream? *The treasure of the eye is elsewhere!* Most artists are still for turning around the hands of the clock, in every sense of the phrase, without having the slightest concern for the spring hidden in the opaque case.

The eye-spring . . . Arshile Gorky – for me the first painter to whom the secret has been completely revealed! Truly the eye was not made to take inventory like an auctioneer, nor to flirt with delusions and false recognitions like a maniac. It was made to cast a lineament, a conducting wire between the most heterogene-ous things. Such a wire, of maximum ductility, should allow us to understand, in a minimum of time, the relationships which connect, with-out possible discharge of continuity, innumer-able physical and mental structures. These re-lationships have been scrambled interminably by false laws of conventional proximity (the apple calls for a pear in the fruit compote) or of scientific classification (for better or worse the lobster and the spider are 'brothers' under the shell). The key of the mental prison can only be found in a break from such absurd manners of perception: the key lies in a free unlimited play of analogies.

Easy-going amateurs will come here for their meagre rewards: in spite of all warning to the contrary they will insist on seeing in these com-positions a still life, a landscape, or a figure instead of daring to face the *hybrid* forms in which all human emotion is precipitated. By 'hybrids' I mean the results provoked in an observer contemplating a natural spectacle with extreme concentration, the results being a com-bination of the spectacle and a flux of childhood and other memories, and the observer being gifted to a rare degree with the grace of emotion. In short it is my concern to emphasize that Gorky is, of all the surrealist artists, the only one who maintains direct contact with nature – sits down to paint *before her*. Furthermore, it is out of the question that he would take the expres-sion of this nature as an end in itself – rightly he demands of her that she provide sensations that can serve as springboards for both knowledge and pleasure in fathoming certain profound

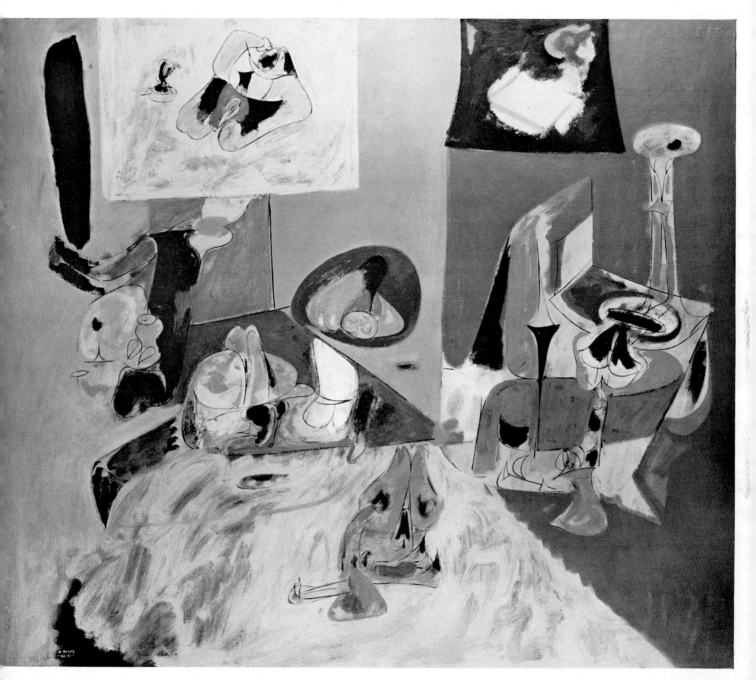

Arshile Gorky *The Calendars*, 1946–7. Oil on canvas 49¾ × 60 in. Lent by Nelson A. Rockefeller, New York

states of mind. Whatever may be the subtle ways by which these states of mind choose to express themselves they stem from the wild and tender personality which Gorky hides, and share the sublime struggle of flowers growing toward the light of day. Here for the first time nature is treated as a cryptogram. The artist has a code by reason of his own sensitive anterior impressions, and can decode nature to reveal the very rhythm of life.

Here is . . . the proof that only absolute purity of means in the service of unalterable freshness of impressions and the gift of unlimited outpouring can empower a leap beyond the ordinary and the known to indicate, with an impeccable arrow of light, a real feeling of liberty.

André Breton, 'Arshile Gorky', Le Surréalisme et la Peinture, *New York, Brentano's, Inc., 1945. (Translation by Julien Levy.)*

In a piece on Arshile Gorky's memorial show – and it was a very little piece indeed – it was mentioned that I was one of his influences. Now that is plain silly. When, about fifteen years ago, I walked into Arshile's studio for the first time, the atmosphere was so beautiful that I got a little dizzy and when I came to, I was bright enough to take the hint immediately. If the bookkeepers think it necessary continuously to make sure of where things and people come from, well then, I come from 36 Union Square [the address of Gorky's studio]. It is incredible to me that other people live there now. I am glad that it is about impossible to get away from his powerful influence. As long as I keep it with myself I'll be doing all right. Sweet Arshile, bless your dear heart.

Willem de Kooning, in a letter to Art News, *Vol.47, January 1949.*

Arshile Gorky
*Dark Green Painting, c.*1947
Oil on canvas 43⅞ × 55⅞ in.
Lent by Mrs H. Gates Lloyd,
Haverford, Pennsylvania

Arshile Gorky *Agony*, 1947. Oil on canvas 40 × 50½ in. Lent by The Museum of Modern Art, New York (A. Conger Goodyear Fund)

Photograph by Lee Bolten

ADOLPH GOTTLIEB

I am ... concerned with the problem of projecting intangible and elusive images that seem to me to have meaning in terms of feeling. The important thing is to transfer the image to the canvas as it appears to me, without distortion. To modify the image would be to falsify it, therefore I must accept it as it is. My criterion is the integrity of the projection.

I frequently hear the question, 'What do these images mean?' This is simply the wrong question. Visual images do not have to conform to either verbal thinking or optical facts. A better question would be, 'Do these images convey any emotional truth?'

This, of course, indicates my belief that art should communicate. However, I have no desire to communicate with everyone, only with those whose thoughts and feelings are related to my own. That is why, even to some pundits, my paintings seem cryptic. Thus when we are solemnly advised to consolidate our gains, to be humanists or to go back to nature, who listens seriously to this whistling in the dark?

Painting values are not just black and white – I prefer innocent impurity to doctrinaire purism, but I prefer the no-content of purism to the shoddy content of social realism. Paint quality is meaningless if it does not express quality of feeling. The idea that a painting is merely an arrangement of lines, colours and forms is boring. Subjective images do not have to have rational association, but the act of painting must be rational, objective, and consciously disciplined. I consider myself a traditionalist, but I believe in the spirit of tradition, not in the restatement of restatements. I love all paintings that look the way I feel.

From a statement by the artist in exhibition catalogue, The New Decade: 35 American Painters and Sculptors, *Whitney Museum of American Art, New York, 1955.*

Adolph Gottlieb *Tournament*, 1951. Oil on canvas $60\frac{1}{4} \times 70\frac{1}{4}$ in. Lent by the artist, New York

Adolph Gottlieb *Side Pull*, 1956. Oil on canvas 50 × 60 in. Lent by Mr and Mrs Clement Greenberg, New York

Adolph Gottlieb *Burst*, 1957. Oil on canvas 96 × 40 in.
Lent by Mr and Mrs Ben Heller, New York

Photograph by Charles Dougherty

PHILIP GUSTON

What is seen and called the picture is what remains – an evidence.

Even as one travels in painting towards a state of 'unfreedom' where only certain things can happen, unaccountably the unknown and free must appear.

Usually I am on a work for a long stretch, until a moment arrives when the air of the arbitrary vanishes and the paint falls into positions that feel destined.

The very matter of painting – its pigment and spaces – is so resistant to the will, so disinclined to assert its plane and remain still.

Painting seems like an impossibility, with only a sign now and then of its own light. Which must be because of the narrow passage from a diagramming to that other state – a corporeality.

In this sense, to paint is a possessing rather than a picturing.

Statement by the artist in exhibition catalogue, 12 *Americans, The Museum of Modern Art, New York,* 1956.

It is not always given to me to know what my pictures 'look like'. I know that I work in a tension provoked by the contradictions I find in painting. I stay on a picture until a time is reached when these paradoxes vanish and conscious choice doesn't exist. I think of painting more in terms of the drama of this process than I do of 'natural' forces.

The ethics involved in 'seeing', as one is painting – the purity of the act, so to speak – is more actual to me than preassumed images or ideas of picture structure. But this is half the story: I doubt if this ethic would be real enough without the 'pull' of the known image for its own 'light', its sense of 'place'.

It is like the impossibility of living entirely in the moment without the tug of memory. The resistance of forms against losing their identities, with, however, their desire to partake of each other, leads finally to a showdown, as they shed their minor relations and confront each other more nakedly. It is almost a state of inertia – these forms, having lived, possess a past and their poise in the visible present on the picture plane must contain the promise of change. Painting, then, for me, is a kind of nagging honesty, with no escape from the repetitious tug-of-war at this intersection.

From an unpublished letter to John I. H. Baur, Curator, Whitney Museum of American Art, New York, in reply to a questionnaire on the role of Nature in abstract art 1957–8.

Philip Guston *Painting*, 1954. Oil on canvas 63¼ × 50⅛ in.
Lent by The Museum of Modern Art, New York (Gift of Philip C. Johnson)

41

Philip Guston *The Clock*, 1957. Oil on canvas 76 × 64 in. Lent by Mrs Sherman J. Sexton, Chicago

Philip Guston *Beggar's Joys*, 1954–5. Oil on canvas $72\frac{1}{8} \times 68\frac{1}{8}$ in. Lent by Boris and Sophie Leavitt, Lana Lobell, Hanover, Pennsylvania

Photograph by Cecil Beaton

GRACE HARTIGAN

Gide said an artist should want only one thing and want it constantly. I want an art that is not 'abstract' and not 'realistic' – I cannot describe the look of this art, but I think I will know it when I see it.

I no longer invite the spectator to walk into my canvases. I want a surface that resists, like a wall, not opens, like a gate.

I have found my 'subject', it concerns that which is vulgar and vital in American modern life, and the possibilities of its transcendence into the beautiful. I do not wish to *describe* my subject matter, or to reflect upon it – I want to distil it until I have its essence. Then the rawness must be resolved into form and unity; without the 'rage for order' how can there be art?

Statement by the artist for exhibition catalogue, 12 Americans, *The Museum of Modern Art, New York,* 1956.

Grace Hartigan *Essex Market*, 1956. Oil on canvas $80\frac{7}{8} \times 69\frac{1}{4}$ in. Lent by Mrs John D. Rockefeller III, New York

Grace Hartigan *City Life*, 1956. Oil on canvas 81 × 98½ in. Lent by Nelson A. Rockefeller, New York

Grace Hartigan *Interior*, '*The Creeks*', 1957. Oil on canvas 90½ × 96 in. Lent by Philip C. Johnson, New Canaan, Connecticut

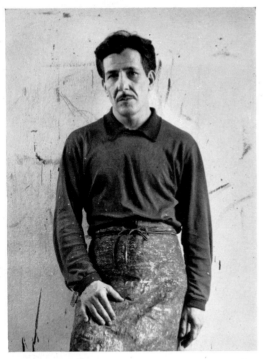

Photograph by Walter Auerbach

FRANZ KLINE

. . . It's not that style has a particular look, it just adds up . . . Somebody will say I have a black-and-white style, or a calligraphic style, but I never started out with that being consciously a style or attitude about painting . . . I don't feel mine is the most modern, contemporary, beyond-the-pale, *gone* kind of painting. But then, I don't have that kind of chuck-the-past attitude. I have very strong feelings about individual paintings and painters past and present.

Now, Bonnard at times seems styleless. Someone said of him that he had the rare ability to forget from one day to another what he had done. He added the next day's experience to it.

. . . In Braque and Gris, they seemed to have an idea of the organization beforehand in their mind. With Bonnard, he is organizing in front of you. You can tell in Léger just when he discovered how to make it like an engine, as John Kane said, being a carpenter, a joiner. What's wrong with that? You see it in Barney Newman too, that he knows what a painting should be. He paints as he thinks *painting* should be, which is pretty heroic.

. . . You instinctively like what you can't do. I like Fra Angelico. I used to try all the time to do those blue eyes that are really blue. Someone once told me to look at Ingres. I loved Daumier and Rembrandt at the time and I was bored when I looked at Ingres. Before long I began to like it. You go through the different phases of liking different guys who are not like you . . .

Tomlin. In a way, they never did much about him and I think it's sad. He didn't start an art school, but he had an influence – his statements were very beautiful. When Pollock talked about painting he didn't usurp anything that wasn't himself. He didn't want to change anything, he wasn't using any outworn attitudes about it, he was always himself. He just wanted to be in it because he loved it . . .

If you're a painter, you're not alone. There's no way to be alone. You think and you care and you're with all the people who care, including the young people who don't know they do yet. Tomlin in his late paintings knew this. Jackson always knew it: that if you meant it enough when you did it, it will mean that much . . . You don't paint the way someone, by observing your life, thinks you *have* to paint, you paint the way you have to in order to *give*, that's life itself, and someone will look and say it is the product of knowing, but it has nothing to do with knowing, it has to do with giving. The question about knowing will naturally be wrong. When you've finished giving, the look surprises you as well as anyone else . . .

Hell, half the world wants to be like Thoreau at Walden worrying about the noise of traffic on the way to Boston; the other half use up their lives being part of that noise. I like the second half. Right?

To be right is the most terrific personal state that nobody is interested in.

From 'Franz Kline Talking' by Frank O'Hara in Evergreen Review, *New York, Vol. 2, No. 6, Autumn* 1958.

Franz Kline *Cardinal*, 1950. Oil on canvas 77½ × 56⅞ in. Lent by Mr and Mrs George Poindexter, New York

Franz Kline *Wanamaker Block*, 1955. Oil on canvas 78¾ × 71¼ in. Lent by Richard Brown Baker, New York

Franz Kline *Accent Grave*, 1955. Oil on canvas 75¼ × 51¾ in. Lent by Mrs John D. Rockefeller III, New York

Photograph by Rudolph Burckhardt

Willem de Koonin[x]
Woman I, 1950–
Oil with charcoal on canv[x]
75⅞ × 58 i[x]
Lent by The Museum [x]
Modern Art, New Yo[x]

WILLEM DE KOONING

Art never seems to make me peaceful or pure. I always seem to be wrapped in the melodrama of vulgarity. I do not think of inside or outside – or of art in general – as a situation of comfort. I know there is a terrific idea there somewhere, but whenever I want to get into it, I get a feeling of apathy and want to lie down and go to sleep. Some painters, including myself, do not care what chair they are sitting on. It does not even have to be a comfortable one. They are too nervous to find out where they ought to sit. They do not want to 'sit in style'. Rather, they have found that painting – any kind of painting, any style of painting – to be painting at all, in fact – is a way of living today, a style of living, so to speak. That is where the form of it lies. It is exactly in its uselessness that it is free. Those artists do not want to conform. They only want to be inspired . . .

That space of science – the space of the physicists – I am truly bored with by now. Their lenses are so thick that seen through them, the space gets more and more melancholy. There seems to be no end to the misery of the scientists' space. All that it contains is billions and billions of hunks of matter, hot or cold, floating around in darkness according to a great design of aimlessness.

The stars *I* think about, if I could fly, I could reach in a few old-fashioned days. But physicists' stars I use as buttons, buttoning up curtains of emptiness. If I stretch my arms next to the rest of myself and wonder where my fingers are – that is all the space I need as a painter.

From 'What Abstract Art Means to Me', symposium held 5 February 1951 at The Museum of Modern Art and printed in the Bulletin, Vol.XVIII, Spring, 1951.

Willem de Kooning *Painting*, 1948. Oil and ripolin enamel on canvas $42\frac{5}{8} \times 56\frac{1}{8}$ in. Lent by The Museum of Modern Art, New York

Willem de Kooning *February*, 1957. Oil on canvas 79½ × 69 in. Lent by Dr and Mrs Edgar Berman, Baltimore, Maryland

Photograph by Hans Namuth

ROBERT MOTHERWELL

When my generation of 'abstract' painters began exhibiting ten years ago, we never expected a general audience, not at least one that would make its presence obvious to us. After many years of genre painting in this country, and the great imports coming from Europe, it would have been unreasonable for us to expect one, no matter what we did; and yet an audience was there all the time, as it was for the cubists in their own time . . . Ten years ago, it seemed that we were embarked upon a solitary voyage, undertaken, I think – in regard to painting – in the belief that 'the essence of life is to be found in the frustrations of the established order'. We were trying to revise modern painting in relation to some of its obvious frustrations, so that painting would represent our sense of reality better. This general tendency each of us followed in his own way . . .

I believe that painters' judgements of painting are first ethical, then aesthetic, the aesthetic judgements flowing from an ethical context . . . Sören Kierkegaard, who did not value painting, was nevertheless very much aware of this distinction in his general analysis of existence. In quite another context, he wrote, 'If anything in the world can teach a man to venture, it is the ethical, which teaches to venture everything for nothing, to risk everything, and also therefore to renounce the flattery of the world-historical . . . the ethical is the absolute, and in all eternity the highest value.' . . . Venturesomeness is only one of the ethical values respected by modern painters. There are many others, integrity, sensuality, sensitivity, knowingness, passion, dedication, sincerity, and so on which taken altogether represent the ethical background of judgement in relation to any given work of modern art.

. . . One has to have an intimate acquaintance with the language of contemporary painting to be able to see the real beauties of it; to see the ethical background is even more difficult. It is a question of consciousness . . .

Without ethical consciousness, a painter is only a decorator.

Without ethical consciousness, the audience is only sensual, one of aesthetes.

From a statement by the artist in a symposium, 'The Creative Artist and His Audience', Perspectives USA, *No.9, Autumn* 1954, *copyright Intercultural Publications Inc.*

Robert Motherwell *Personage with Yellow Ochre and White*, 1947. Oil on canvas 72 × 54 in.
Lent by The Museum of Modern Art, New York (Gift of Mr and Mrs Samuel M. Kootz)

Robert Motherwell *Elegy for the Spanish Republic XXXV*, 1954–8. Oil on canvas 80 × 100¼ in.
Lent by Mr and Mrs Albert Newman, Chicago

Robert Motherwell *The Voyage*, 1949. Oil and tempera on paper on composition board 48 × 94 in.
Lent by The Museum of Modern Art, New York (Gift of Mrs John D. Rockefeller 3rd)

BARNETT NEWMAN

It is precisely this death image, the grip of geometry that has to be confronted.

In a world of geometry, geometry itself has become our moral crisis. And it will not be resolved by jazzed-up kicks but only by the answer of no geometry of any kind. Unless we face up to it and discover a new image based on new principles, there is no hope for freedom.

Can anyone, therefore, take seriously the mock aesthetic war that the art journalists and their artist friends have been waging against the new Pyramid – while they sit in it under a canopy of triangulation – with their feeble frenzy-weapons of the hootchy-cootchy dancer?

I realize that my paintings have no link with, nor any basis in, the art of World War I with its principles of geometry – that tie it into the nineteenth century. To reject Cubism or Purism, whether it is Picasso's or Mondrian's, only to end up with the collage scheme of free associated forms, whether it is Miró's or Malevich's, is to be caught in the same geometric trap. Only an art free from any kind of the geometry principles of World War I, only an art of no-geometry can be a new beginning.

Nor can I find it by building a wall of lights; nor in the dead infinity of silence; nor in the painting performance, as if it were an instrument of pure energy full of a hollow biologic rhetoric.

Painting, like passion, is a living voice, which, when I hear it, I must let speak, unfettered.

Statement by the artist for the present exhibition, 1958.

Barnett Newman *Concord*, 1949.
Oil on canvas 90 × 54 in.
Lent by Mrs Betty Parsons, New York

Barnett Newman *Abraham*, 1949. Oil on canvas 84 × 35½ in.
Lent by Betty Parsons Gallery, New York

Barnett Newman *Adam*, 1951–2. Oil on canvas 95⅜ × 79⅜ in. Lent by Mr and Mrs Ben Heller, New York

Photograph by Hans Namuth

JACKSON POLLOCK

My painting does not come from the easel. I hardly ever stretch my canvas before painting. I prefer to tack the unstretched canvas to the hard wall or the floor. I need the resistance of a hard surface. On the floor I am more at ease. I feel nearer, more a part of the painting, since this way I can walk around it, work from the four sides, and literally be *in* the painting. This is akin to the method of the Indian sand painters of the West . . .

When I am *in* my painting, I'm not aware of what I'm doing. It is only after a sort of 'get acquainted' period that I see what I have been about. I have no fears about making changes, destroying the image, etc., because the painting has a life of its own. I try to let it come through. It is only when I lose contact with the painting that the result is a mess. Otherwise there is pure harmony, an easy give and take, and the painting comes out well.

From a statement by the artist in Possibilities, *I, Winter 1947–8 ('Problems of Contemporary Art', No.4, copyright Wittenborn Inc.)*

The attention focused on his immediate qualities – the unconventional materials and methods of working, the scale and immediate splendour of much of his work – has left largely untouched the forces that compel him to work in the manner that he does. Why the tension and complexity of line, the violently interwoven movement so closely knit as almost to induce the static quality of perpetual motion, the careful preservation of the picture's surface plane linked with an intricately rich interplay upon the canvas, the rupture with traditional compositional devices that produces, momentarily, the sense that the picture could be continued indefinitely in any direction?

His painting confronts us with a visual concept organically evolved from a belief in the unity that underlies the phenomena among which we live. Void and solid, human action and inertia, are metamorphosed and refined into the energy that sustains them and is their common denominator. An ocean's tides and a personal nightmare, the bursting of a bubble, and the communal clamour for a victim are as inextricably meshed in the coruscation and darkness of his work as they are in actuality. His forms and textures germinate, climax and decline, coalesce and dissolve across the canvas. The picture surface, with no depth of recognizable space or sequence of known time, gives us the never-ending present. We are presented with a visualization of that remorseless consolation – in the end is the beginning.

New visions demand new techniques: Pollock's use of unexpected materials and scales is the direct result of his concepts and of the organic intensity with which he works, an intensity that involves, in its complete identification of the artist with his work, a denial of the accident.

From introduction by Alfonso Ossorio in exhibition catalogue, Jackson Pollock 1951, *Betty Parsons Gallery, New York; also quoted in* 15 Americans, *The Museum of Modern Art, New York, 1952.*

Jackson Pollock *Number 27*, 1951. Duco on canvas $55\frac{3}{4} \times 75\frac{1}{4}$ in. Lent by Sidney Janis Gallery, New York

Jackson Pollock *Number* 8, 1949. Duco and aluminium on canvas 34 × 71½ in. Lent by Mr and Mrs Roy R. Neuberger, New York, New York

Jackson Pollock *Number* 12, 1952
Oil on canvas 101⅞ × 89 in
Lent by Nelson A. Rockefeller
New York

MARK ROTHKO

Rothko's development has been consistently accomplished through the exclusion of *intricacies* of form. From his early expressionist paintings, through surrealist images, fantasies of undersea plant-life and cephalopods, monotone wash-drawings, his development has, at each new stage, abandoned some visual element to gain a spiritual one. In the late 'forties, his undersea forms began to lose their contours, and patches of colour, still suggesting a submarine existence, began to appear on horizontal canvases. The patches became larger, closer in value, more luminous in hue. They lost their biomorphic shapes and began to arrange themselves in hazy, dignified, rectangular formations. His canvases became vertical although retaining their horizontal souls. The formations continued to grow in size, expanding into each other's territory; edges disappeared as they met and overlapped, until, finally, in his present work, it is as though the shapes got bigger than the canvas – their boundaries are outside it – and what is left is simply the *process* of expansion.

From Elaine de Kooning, 'Kline and Rothko: Two Americans in Action', 1958 Art News Annual.

The progression of a painter's work, as it travels in time from point to point, will be toward clarity: toward the elimination of all obstacles between the painter and the idea, and between the idea and the observer. As examples of such obstacles, I give (among others) memory, history, or geometry, which are swamps of generalization from which one might pull out parodies of ideas (which are ghosts) but never an idea in itself. To achieve this clarity is, inevitably, to be understood.

From a statement by the artist in The Tiger's Eye, *October 1949; also quoted in exhibition catalogue, 15 Americans, The Museum of Modern Art, New York, 1952.*

Mark Rothko *Number* 10, 1950.
Oil on canvas 90⅜ × 57⅛ in.
Lent by The Museum of Modern Art,
New York (Gift of Philip C. Johnson)

Mark Rothko *Tan and Black on Red*, 1957
Oil on canvas 69⅜ × 53⅜ in. Lent by
Mr and Mrs I. Donald Grossman
New York

Mark Rothko *The Black and the White*, 1956
Oil on canvas 94 × 53¾ in. Lent by
Dr and Mrs Frank Stanton, New York

Photograph by Lee Boltin

THEODOROS STAMOS

Considering that so much has been and will be written on art, in the last analysis, painting at its best consists of truth to one's paint, to one's self and one's time, and most of all to one's God and one's dream.

Statement by the artist for the present exhibition, 1958.

72

Theodoros Stamos *White Field, Number* 2, 1957. Oil on canvas 60 × 72⅜ in.
Lent by Mr and Mrs Paul Rankine, Bethesda, Maryland

Theodoros Stamos *High Snow, Low Sun, Number* 3, 1957. Oil on canvas $56\frac{1}{2} \times 56\frac{3}{4}$ in.
Lent by André Emmerich Gallery, New York

Theodoros Stamos *Sun Games, Number* 2, 1958. Oil on canvas $70\frac{7}{8} \times 61$ in. Lent by Mr and Mrs Guy A. Weill, Scarsdale, New York

From the most ancient times the artist has been expected to perpetuate the values of his contemporaries. The record is mainly one of frustration, sadism, superstition, and the will to power. What greatness of life crept into the story came from sources not yet fully understood, and the temples of art which burden the landscape of nearly every city are a tribute to the attempt to seize this elusive quality and stamp it out . . .

We are now committed to an unqualified act, not illustrating outworn myths or contemporary alibis. One must accept total responsibility for what he executes. And the measure of his greatness will be in the depth of his insight and his courage in realizing his own vision.

Demands for communication are both presumptuous and irrelevant. The observer usually will see what his fears and hopes and learning teach him to see. But if he can escape these demands that hold up a mirror to himself, then perhaps some of the implications of the work may be felt.

From a letter by the artist dated February 5, 1952, quoted in exhibition catalogue, 15 Americans, *The Museum of Modern Art, New York, 1952.*

Clyfford Still *Number* 2, 1
Oil on canvas 91¾ × 68
Lent by Mr and Mrs Ben He
New Y

Clyfford Still *Number* 3, 1951. Oil on canvas 46¾ × 37⅞ in. Lent by Mrs Betty Parsons, New York

Clyfford Still *Painting*, 1951. Oil on canvas 94 × 82 in.
Lent by The Museum of Modern Art, New York
(Blanchette Rockefeller Fund)

79

Bradley Walker Tomlin *Number 9:*
In Praise of Gertrude Stein,
1950. Oil on canvas 49 × 102¼ in.
Lent by The Museum of Modern Art,
New York (Gift of
Mrs John D. Rockefeller III)

Photograph by Rudolph Burckhardt

BRADLEY WALKER TOMLIN

Formulation of belief has a way of losing its brightness and of fencing one in. The artist having found, and publicly declared, what seem to be the answers, will then in all likelihood swear to protect them, as if upon oath, since stated beliefs, like certificates in the anterooms of practitioners, imply the authority to pursue a predictable course of action. Doubts, however, creep in. One peers at the old diplomas more closely, speculating vaguely as to the guarantee in time the authoritative body might have had the temerity to fix upon . . .

Moved deeply by a painting, the spectator may say, the artist has convinced me. This is really painting, it is the way it should be done. One can believe in paintings, as one can believe in miracles, for paintings, like miracles, possess an inner logic which is inescapable. But this again is to believe after the fact, which is merely to believe in the concrete.

What does the artist himself believe in, having produced his miracle? Does he feel that he is now in the clear, that in the future the canvases will be solved without pain? His intentions presumably are clear and it is possible to believe in the reality of intentions, good or bad. Can one be sure, however, that in different situations, intentions can be identical? Does the artist find that the seemingly effortless structure, which he has evolved with total clarity, tends on repetition to escape him? That in spite of the production of masterpieces, art itself remains infinitely mysterious and that the work in progress is merely a kind of hall rack on which he has hung various nicely woven articles of clothing: jackets shabbily elegant, old hats battered to his image. Confronted by the cast of his own mind he says, it is at least mine. Yet the jacket he has slipped into binds slightly under the armpits. Umbrellas and old walking sticks clatter to the floor.

Unpublished statement, presumably written in 1950 for Modern Artists in America, *Vol.II (Robert Motherwell, editor).*

Bradley Walker Tomlin, like his paintings, possessed a tensile – and at times precarious – balance that covered an anguished sense of alternatives. IIis tone, muted, graded, could change to caprice.

Wearied by the already experienced and the flaccid, yet bound by a gift of proportion, his spontaneity was earned. The reworked and scored painting surface gradually exposed vein and nerve, and this was the cost. The stroke, which tends to leap, is nevertheless held on the plane – like the seal on a letter. Since his temperament insisted on the impossible pleasure of controlling and being free at the same moment, his plasticity and its demands are quickening.

Tomlin's passion did not distort the surface: an innate feeling for amounts prevented him from becoming an 'expressionist'. Often wry, he never lost his fineness of edge. In the more 'intimate' or 'written' paintings thought became the hand, releasing lean rhythms that did not forget the resistance of an earlier cubist space. By choice denying himself certain luxuries of colour, he would use, perhaps, a drab olive, a mustard, an old white.

An heraldic elegy is his form, and this elegance is as nimble as it is grave.

Note on the artist by Philip Guston in exhibition catalogue, Bradley Walker Tomlin, *Whitney Museum of American Art, New York*, 1957.

Bradley Walker Tomlin *Number 20*, 1949. Oil with charcoal on canvas 86 × 80¼ in. Lent by The Museum of Modern Art, New York (Gift of Philip C. Johnson)

Bradley Walker Tomlin *Number* 15, 1953. Oil on canvas 46 × 76 in. Lent by Mr and Mrs Ben Heller, New York

JACK TWORKOV

My hope is to confront the picture without a ready technique or a prepared attitude – a condition which is nevertheless never completely attainable; to have no programme and, necessarily then, no preconceived style. To paint no Tworkovs. It does not mean I can face the canvas with an empty head and an empty heart. In such an event I go to sleep. Does one not need to put limits around oneself to keep from being overwhelmed by the stream of art? The fashioned person is already limited enough – the hope is to be fashioned by the work. The task of painting is to discover and squeeze out, from all the forces streaming through it, all that is not necessary. Such impurities as remain are finally present to lend coherence to the process.

I am against the negativism which intellectuals foster that every advance, even where that is not simply an illusion, takes place in an atmosphere of quarrel with the past, and dissidence from the present. But I abhor the adulators, the masochistic art-victims on their knees to 'great masters'. Their chief passion is to put everything in chains.

I offer to thoughtful artists this quotation: 'The man who reduces [the] encounter between the cosmos of history and its eternally new chaos, between Zeus and Dionysus, to the formula of the "antagonism between fathers and sons", has never beheld it in his spirit. Zeus the Father does not stand for a generation but for a world, for the Olympic, the formed world; the world of history faces a particular generation, which is the world of nature renewed again and again, always without history.'*

* From Martin Buber, *Between Man and Man* (London, The Macmillan Company, 1947).

From a statement by the artist for catalogue of an exhibition of his paintings, Stable Gallery, New York, 1957.

Jack Tworkov, *Cradle*, 1956. Oil on canvas 72¼ × 64¼ in.
Lent by Mr and Mrs William Calfee, Washington, D.C.

Jack Tworkov *Blue Cradle*, 1956. Oil on canvas 72 × 64 in. Lent by Mr and Mrs Donald M. Blinken, New York

Jack Tworkov *Transverse*, 1957–8. Oil on canvas 72 × 76 in. Lent by Mr and Mrs Ben Heller, New York

CATALOGUE

The data contained in the biographical notes for each artist have been compiled from the most reliable sources available and wherever possible have been checked with the artist himself. All one-man shows for each artist have been listed. The section *Included in:* lists major group exhibitions in the United States in which the artist was represented by two or more works. *Group exhibitions outside the United States:* lists all such exhibitions in which the artist was represented, even by a single work.

Many of the biographies refer to the 'WPA Federal Art Project'. This was part of the Works Progress Administration, a nation-wide programme established by the United States Government in 1935 to combat unemployment resulting from the Great Depression.

Unframed dimensions given; height precedes width. The arrangement of the items is chronological. Parentheses indicate that dates are not shown on the work itself. ★Works marked with a star are illustrated.

WILLIAM BAZIOTES

Biography: Born 1912, Pittsburgh, Pennsylvania; grew up in Reading, Pennsylvania. To New York, 1933; studied at National Academy of Design, 1933–6. Worked on WPA Federal Art Project, New York, as teacher 1936–8, on easel painting project 1938–41. In 1948, founder with Motherwell, Newman, and Rothko, of school on East 8th Street, New York, 'Subjects of the Artist', out of which grew 'The Club' with weekly meetings of *avant-garde* artists. Taught at Brooklyn Museum Art School, New York, 1949–52; New York University, 1949–52; People's Art Center of the Museum of Modern Art, New York, 1950–2; Hunter College, New York, 1952 to present. Lives in New York.

One-man shows: Art of This Century (Peggy Guggenheim), New York, 1944; Galerie Maeght, Paris, 1947; Kootz Gallery, New York, yearly 1946–8, 1950–4, 1956, 1958.

Included in: 15 *Americans*, The Museum of Modern Art, New York, 1952; *The New Decade*, Whitney Museum of American Art, New York, shown thereafter in San Francisco, Los Angeles, Colorado Springs and St Louis, 1955–6.

Group Exhibitions outside the United States of America: Kootz Gallery Group, Galerie Maeght, Paris, 1947; *American Vanguard Art for Paris*, Galerie de France, Paris, 1952 (shown at Sidney Janis Gallery, New York, 1951–2); U.S. Representation, II Bienal, São Paulo, 1953; U.S. Representation, Tenth Inter-American Conference, Caracas, 1954; *Modern Art in the United States: Selections from the Collections of the Museum of Modern Art, New York*, Paris, Zurich, Barcelona, Frankfurt, London, The Hague, Vienna, and Belgrade, 1955–6.

★**1** *Dwarf* 1947
Oil on canvas $42 \times 36\frac{1}{8}$ in.
Lent by The Museum of Modern Art, New York
(A. Conger Goodyear Fund)

★**2** *Primeval Landscape* 1953
Oil on canvas 60×72 in.
Lent by the Philadelphia Museum of Art, Philadelphia
(Samuel S. Fleisher Art Memorial)

★**3** *Pompeii* 1956
Oil on canvas 60×48 in.
Lent by The Museum of Modern Art, New York
(Mrs Louise Smith Fund)

4 *Red Landscape* 1957
Oil on canvas $72\frac{1}{4} \times 60\frac{1}{4}$ in.
Lent by The Minneapolis Institute of Arts, Minneapolis
(Bigelow Fund)

JAMES BROOKS

Biography: Born 1906, St Louis, Missouri; grew up in various parts of the West. In Dallas, Texas, 1916–26; attended Southern Methodist University, Dallas, 1923–5. To New York, 1926; studied at Art Students' League with Kimon Nicolaides and Boardman Robinson, 1927–30. Worked on WPA Federal Art Project, New York, 1938–42, painting murals at Queensborough Public Library, Woodside Branch, 1938, and International Overseas Air Terminal, La Guardia Airport, 1942. Served in U.S.Army, 1942–5, in Egypt and Middle East. Fifth prize, 1952 Pittsburgh International Exhibition of Painting, Carnegie Institute, Pittsburgh, Pennsylvania. Taught at Columbia University, New York, 1946–8; visiting critic of painting, Yale University, 1955–6. Teacher, Pratt Institute, Brooklyn, 1948 to present. Lives in New York and Springs, Long Island, New York.

One-man shows: Peridot Gallery, New York, yearly 1950–3; Miller-Pollard Gallery, Seattle, 1952; Area Arts, San

Francisco, 1953; Grace Borgenicht Gallery, New York, 1954; Stable Gallery, New York, 1957.

Included in: The New Decade, Whitney Museum of American Art, New York, shown thereafter in San Francisco, Los Angeles, Colorado Springs and St Louis, 1955–6; 12 *Americans*, The Museum of Modern Art, New York, 1956.

Group Exhibitions outside the United States of America: American Vanguard Art for Paris, Galerie de France, Paris, 1952 (shown at Sidney Janis Gallery, New York, 1951–2); *Recent American Watercolors*, five cities in France, 1956–7; U.S. Representation, IV Bienal, São Paulo, 1957.

5 *R* 1953
Oil on canvas $82\frac{1}{2} \times 88$ in.
Lent by Stable Gallery, New York

*6 *Qualm* 1954
Oil on canvas $61 \times 57\frac{1}{8}$ in.
Lent by The Museum of Modern Art, New York
(Gift of Mrs Bliss Parkinson)

*7 *Jackson* (1956)
Oil on canvas $66\frac{3}{4} \times 69\frac{3}{4}$ in.
Lent by Nelson A. Rockefeller, New York

*8 *Karrig* 1956
Oil on canvas $79\frac{1}{8} \times 73\frac{1}{2}$ in.
Lent by Stable Gallery, New York

9 *Bixby* 1958
Oil on canvas 51×66 in.
Lent by Stable Gallery, New York

SAM FRANCIS

Biography: Born 1923, San Mateo, California. University of California, Berkeley, 1941–3; B.A. 1949, M.A. 1950. Served in U.S. Army Air Force, 1943–5. Began painting in San Francisco, 1945. To Paris, 1950. Painted murals for Kunsthalle, Basle, 1956–8. To Japan, 1957; painted mural for Sofu School of Flower Arrangements, Tokyo. Lives in Paris.

One-man shows: Galerie Nina Dausset, Paris, 1952; Galerie Rive Droite, Paris, 1955, 1956; Martha Jackson Gallery, New York, 1956, 1957; Gimpel Fils, London, 1957; Kornfeld and Klipstein, Berne, 1957; Toyoko Department Store Gallery, Tokyo, 1957; Kintetsu Department Store Gallery, Osaka, 1957.

Included in: 12 *Americans*, The Museum of Modern Art, New York, 1956.

Group Exhibitions outside the United States of America: Salon de Mai, Paris, 1950; Galerie Nina Dausset, Paris, 1951; *Signifiants de l'Informal*, Studio Paul Facchetti, Paris (presented by Michel Tapié), 1952; *Un Art Autre*, Studio Paul Facchetti, Paris (presented by Michel Tapié), 1953; *Opposing Forces*, Institute of Contemporary Arts, London, 1953; Galerie Rive Droite, Paris, 1954; Galleria Spazio,

Rome, 1954, 1955; *Tendances Actuelles*, Kunsthalle, Berne, 1955; Gallery Samlaren, Stockholm, 1955; U.S. Representation, 4th International Art Exhibition, Japan, nine cities 1957 (receiving one of five prizes awarded non-Japanese artists); *Exploration of Paint*, Arthur Tooth and Sons Ltd, London, 1957; *New Trends in Painting*, Arts Council Gallery, London, 1957.

*10 *Big Red* (1953)
Oil on canvas 119×76 in.
Lent by The Museum of Modern Art, New York
(Gift of Mr and Mrs David Rockefeller)

*11 *Black in Red* (1953)
Oil on canvas $77 \times 51\frac{1}{4}$ in.
Lent by The Museum of Modern Art, New York
(Blanchette Rockefeller Fund)

*12 *Blue and Black* (1954)
Oil on canvas $77 \times 51\frac{1}{2}$ in.
Lent by E. J. Power, London

13 *Arcueil* 1956
Oil on canvas $82 \times 76\frac{1}{2}$ in.
Lent by Martha Jackson Gallery, New York

ARSHILE GORKY

Biography: Born 1905, Hayotz Dzore, Turkish Armenia. During World War I, emigrated to Russian Transcaucasia. Studied at Polytechnic Institute, Tiflis, 1916–18. To U.S.A. 1920; lived first in Watertown, Massachusetts, then Providence; attended night classes at Rhode Island School of Design. To Boston, 1923; attended New School of Design, 1923, and instructed in life class, 1924. To New York, 1925, brief attendance at National Academy of Design. Taught at New York School of Design, then Grand Central School of Art, 1926–31. Worked on WPA Federal Art Project, New York, 1936–8, painting murals for Newark Airport, New Jersey (no longer in existence). Mural for Aviation Building, New York World's Fair, 1939. Organized class in camouflage at Grand Central School of Art, New York, 1942. From 1943 spent part of each year in Virginia and Connecticut until death by suicide, 1948.

One-man shows: Guild Art Gallery, New York, 1932, 1935 (drawings only), 1936; Mellon Galleries, Philadelphia, 1934; Boyer Art Galleries, Philadelphia, 1935 (drawings only), Boyer Gallery, New York, 1938; San Francisco Museum of Art, 1941; Julien Levy Gallery, New York, 1945, 1946, 1947 (drawings only), 1948; Kootz Gallery, New York, 1947, 1950, 1951 (drawings only). Memorial exhibition, Whitney Museum of American Art, New York, shown thereafter in Minneapolis and San Francisco, 1951. Art Museum, Princeton University, 1952; Paul Kantor Gallery, Los Angeles, 1952; Sidney Janis Gallery, New York, 1953, 1955 (drawings only), 1957.

Included in: An Exhibition of Work by 46 *Painters and Sculptors under 35 Years of Age*, The Museum of Modern

Art, New York, 1930; *Abstract Painting in America*, Whitney Museum of American Art, New York, 1935; 14 *Americans*, The Museum of Modern Art, New York, 1946.

Group Exhibitions outside the United States of America: La Pintura Contemporánea Norteamericana, New York, Havana, Mexico City, Caracas, Bogotá, Quito, Lima, Santiago, Rio de Janeiro, Montevideo, Buenos Aires, 1941; *Le Surréalisme en 1947, Exposition Internationale du Surréalisme présentée par André Breton et Marcel Duchamp*, Galerie Maeght, Paris, 1947; U.S. Representation, XXIV Biennale, Venice, 1948; U.S. Representation, XXV Biennale, Venice, 1950; *American Vanguard Art for Paris*, Galerie de France, Paris, 1952 (shown at Sidney Janis Gallery, New York, 1951–2); U.S. Representation, 2nd International Contemporary Art Exhibition, India, five cities, 1953; 12 *Modern American Painters and Sculptors*, Paris, Zurich, Düsseldorf, Stockholm, Helsinki, and Oslo, 1953–4; U.S. Representation, Tenth Inter-American Conference, Caracas, 1954; *Modern Art in the United States: Selections from the Collections of the Museum of Modern Art, New York*, Paris, Zurich, Barcelona, Frankfurt, London, The Hague, Vienna, and Belgrade, 1955–6; U.S. Representation, 3rd International Contemporary Art Exhibition, India, six cities, 1957.

14 *Diary of a Seducer* 1945
Oil on canvas 50 × 62 in.
Lent by Mr and Mrs William A. M. Burden, New York

*15 *The Calendars* 1946–7
Oil on canvas 49¾ × 60 in.
Lent by Nelson A. Rockefeller, New York

*16 *Agony* 1947
Oil on canvas 40 × 50½ in.
Lent by The Museum of Modern Art, New York
(A. Conger Goodyear Fund)

*17 *Dark Green Painting* (c.1947)
Oil on canvas 43⅞ × 55⅞ in.
Lent by Mrs H. Gates Lloyd, Haverford, Pennsylvania

18 *The Limit* 1947
Oil on paper over burlap 50¾ × 62½ in.
Lent by Sidney Janis Gallery, New York

19 *Soft Night* 1947
Oil on canvas 38 × 50 in.
Lent by Mr and Mrs John Stephan, Greenwich, Connecticut

ADOLPH GOTTLIEB

Biography: Born 1903, New York. Studied with John Sloan and Robert Henri at Art Students League, 1920, 1923; worked independently in Paris, Berlin, and Munich, 1921–2. Founding member, with Rothko, of 'The Ten' group, New York, 1935. To Arizona, 1937. Mural commissioned by U.S. Treasury Department, Section of Fine Arts, for Post Office, Yerington, Nevada, 1939. To New York, 1939. Designed ark curtains for synagogue of Congregation B'nai Israel, Millburn, New Jersey, 1951, and for Temple Beth El, Springfield, Massachusetts, 1953; stained-glass façade and mural for Park Avenue Synagogue Community Center, New York, 1955. Teacher, Pratt Institute, Brooklyn, 1955 to present. Lives in New York.

One-man shows: Dudensing Gallery, New York, 1930; Uptown Gallery, New York, 1934; Theodore A. Kohn Gallery, New York, 1934; Artists' Gallery, New York, 1940, 1943; Wakefield Gallery, New York, 1944; 67 Gallery (Howard Putzel), New York, 1945; Nierendorf Gallery, New York, 1945; Kootz Gallery, New York, 1947 (two shows) and yearly 1950–4; Jacques Seligmann Gallery, New York, 1949; Area Arts, San Francisco, 1953; Bennington College, Bennington, Vermont, 1954; Williams College, Williamstown, Massachusetts, 1954; Martha Jackson Gallery, New York, 1957; Jewish Museum, New York, 1957; André Emmerich Gallery, New York, 1958.

Included in: The New Decade, Whitney Museum of American Art, New York, shown thereafter in San Francisco, Los Angeles, Colorado Springs and St Louis, 1955–6.

Group Exhibitions outside the United States of America: *Kootz Gallery Group*, Galerie Maeght, Paris, 1947; *American Vanguard Art for Paris*, Galerie de France, Paris, 1952 (shown at Sidney Janis Gallery, New York, 1951–2); U.S. Representation, 1st International Art Exhibition, Japan, five cities, 1952; U.S. Representation, 3rd International Art Exhibition, Japan, eight cities, 1955; U.S. Representation, 3rd International Contemporary Art Exhibition, India, six cities, 1957; 75 *Paintings from the Solomon R. Guggenheim Museum, New York*, London, The Hague, Helsinki, Rome, Cologne, Paris, 1957–8.

*20 *Tournament* 1951
Oil on canvas 60¼ × 70¼ in.
Lent by the artist, New York

21 *Black, Blue, Red* 1956
Oil on canvas 72 × 50 in.
Lent by the artist, New York

22 *Red at Night* 1956
Oil on canvas 72 × 96 in.
Lent by the artist, New York

*23 *Side Pull* 1956
Oil on canvas 50 × 60 in.
Lent by Mr and Mrs Clement Greenberg, New York

*24 *Burst* (1957)
Oil on canvas 96 × 40 in.
Lent by Mr and Mrs Ben Heller, New York

PHILIP GUSTON

Biography: Born 1913, Montreal, Canada. To U.S.A., 1916; grew up in Los Angeles. Three months at Otis Art Institute, Los Angeles; otherwise self-taught. To Mexico, 1934–5; to New York, 1935. Worked on WPA Federal Art Project, New York, 1935–40, painting murals for Federal Works Agency Building, New York World's Fair, 1939, Queensbridge Housing Project, 1940, and other projects. Murals commissioned by U.S. Treasury Department, Section of Fine Arts, Post Office, Commerce, Georgia, 1938, and Social Security Building, Washington, D.C., 1942. Travelled in Italy, Spain, France, 1947–9, on Guggenheim Fellowship, Prix de Rome and grant from American Academy of Arts and Letters. Taught at State University of Iowa, 1941–5; Washington University, St Louis, 1945–7; New York University, 1950 to present. Lives in New York and West Hurley, New York.

One-man shows: State University of Iowa, 1944; Midtown Galleries, New York, 1945; School of the Museum of Fine Arts, Boston, 1947; Munson-Williams-Proctor Institute, Utica, New York, 1947; University of Minnesota, Minneapolis, 1950; Peridot Gallery, New York, 1952; Egan Gallery, New York, 1953; Sidney Janis Gallery, New York, 1956, 1958.

Included in: 12 *Americans,* The Museum of Modern Art, New York, 1956.

Group Exhibitions outside the United States of America: American Vanguard Art for Paris, Galerie de France, Paris, 1952 (shown at Sidney Janis Gallery, New York, 1951–2); *Modern Art in the United States: Selections from the Collections of The Museum of Modern Art, New York,* Paris, Zurich, Barcelona, Frankfurt, London, The Hague, Vienna, and Belgrade, 1955–6; *Recent American Watercolors,* five cities in France, 1956–7; U.S. Representation, IV Bienal, São Paulo, 1957.

★**25** *Painting* 1954
Oil on canvas 63¼ × 50⅛ in.
Lent by The Museum of Modern Art, New York
(Gift of Philip C. Johnson)

★**26** *Beggar's Joys* 1954–5
Oil on canvas 72⅛ × 68⅛ in.
Lent by Boris and Sophie Leavitt, Lana Lobell, Hanover, Pennsylvania

 27 *The Room* 1954–5
Oil on canvas 72 × 60 in.
Lent by Mrs Leo Castelli, New York

★**28** *The Clock* 1957
Oil on canvas 76 × 64 in.
Lent by Mrs Sherman J. Sexton, Chicago

 29 *The Mirror* 1957
Oil on canvas 68⅜ × 61 in.
Lent by Mrs Bliss Parkinson, New York

GRACE HARTIGAN

Biography: Born 1922, Newark, New Jersey; grew up in Millburn, New Jersey. In California, 1941–2. Worked from about 1942–7 as mechanical draughtsman in war industry in Bloomfield and Newark, New Jersey; New York; and White Plains, New York. Studied painting in night classes of Isaac Lane Muse, Newark, New Jersey. To New York about 1945; one year in Mexico, 1948–9. Lives in New York.

One-man shows: Tibor de Nagy Gallery, New York, yearly 1951–5, 1957; Vassar College Art Gallery, Poughkeepsie, New York, 1954.

Included in: 12 *Americans,* The Museum of Modern Art, New York, 1956.

Group Exhibitions outside the United States of America: Modern Art in the United States: Selections from the Collections of The Museum of Modern Art, New York, Paris, Zurich, Barcelona, Frankfurt, London, The Hague, Vienna, and Belgrade, 1955–6; U.S. Representation, 3rd International Contemporary Art Exibition, India, six cities, 1957; U.S. Representation, 4th International Art Exhibition, Japan, nine cities, 1957; U.S. Representation, IV Bienal, São Paulo, 1957.

 30 *River Bathers* 1953
Oil on canvas 69⅜ × 88¾ in.
Lent by The Museum of Modern Art, New York
(Given anonymously)

★**31** *City Life* 1956
Oil on canvas 81 × 98½ in.
Lent by Nelson A. Rockefeller, New York

★**32** *Essex Market* 1956
Oil on canvas 80⅞ × 69¼ in.
Lent by Mrs John D. Rockefeller III, New York

★**33** *Interior, 'The Creeks'* 1957
Oil on canvas 90½ × 96 in.
Lent by Philip C. Johnson, New Canaan, Connecticut

 34 *On Orchard Street* 1957
Oil on canvas 70½ × 80¼ in.
Lent by Mr and Mrs Patrick B. McGinnis, Boston, Massachusetts

FRANZ KLINE

Biography: Born 1910, Wilkes-Barre, Pennsylvania; grew up in Philadelphia. School of Fine and Applied Arts, Boston University, 1931–5; Heatherly's Art School, London, 1937–8. To New York, 1938. First exhibited in National Academy of Design Annuals, New York, yearly 1942–5. Taught at Black Mountain College, North Carolina, summer 1952; Pratt Institute, Brooklyn, New York, 1953–4; Philadelphia Museum School of Art, 1954. Lives in New York.

One-man shows: Egan Gallery, New York, 1950, 1951, 1954;

Margaret Brown Gallery, Boston, 1952; Institute of Design, Chicago, 1954; Allan Frumkin Gallery, Chicago, 1954; Sidney Janis Gallery, New York, 1956, 1958; La Tartaruga Gallery, Rome, 1958.

Included in: The New Decade, Whitney Museum of American Art, New York, shown thereafter in San Francisco, Los Angeles, Colorado Springs and St Louis, 1955–6; *12 Americans*, The Museum of Modern Art, New York, 1956.

Group Exhibitions outside the United States of America; American Vanguard Art for Paris, Galerie de France, Paris, 1952 (shown at Sidney Janis Gallery, New York, 1951–2); U.S. Representation, Tenth Inter-American Conference, Caracas, 1954; *Modern Art in the United States: Selections from the Collections of The Museum of Modern Art, New York*, Paris, Zurich, Barcelona, Frankfurt, London, The Hague, Vienna, and Belgrade, 1955–6; U.S. Representation, XXVIII Biennale, Venice, 1956; *Recent American Watercolors*, five cities in France, 1956–7; *75 Paintings from the Solomon R. Guggenheim Museum, New York*, London, The Hague, Helsinki, Rome, Cologne, Paris, 1957–8.

*35 *Cardinal* 1950
Oil on canvas $77\frac{1}{2} \times 56\frac{7}{8}$ in.
Lent by Mr and Mrs George Poindexter, New York

36 *Chief* (1950)
Oil on canvas $58\frac{3}{8} \times 73\frac{1}{2}$ in.
Lent by The Museum of Modern Art, New York
(Gift of Mr and Mrs David M. Solinger)

*37 *Accent Grave* 1955
Oil on canvas $75\frac{1}{4} \times 51\frac{3}{4}$ in.
Lent by Mrs John D. Rockefeller III, New York

*38 *Wanamaker Block* (1955)
Oil on canvas $78\frac{3}{4} \times 71\frac{1}{4}$ in.
Lent by Richard Brown Baker, New York

39 *Garcia* 1957
Oil on canvas $95 \times 79\frac{5}{8}$ in.
Lent by Sidney Janis Gallery, New York

WILLEM DE KOONING

Biography: Born 1904, Rotterdam, Holland. Apprenticed when 12 to painting and decorating firm. In 1919 apprenticed to the painter Bernard Romein, and attended night classes at Rotterdam Academy of Fine Arts; graduated 1924. Later attended art schools in Brussels and Antwerp. To U.S.A. 1926; house-painting and decorating, free-lance commercial art, stage designing. Worked on WPA Federal Art Project, New York, 1935–6, easel and mural divisions. Painted mural for the New York World's Fair, 1939. Taught at Yale University, 1952–3. Lives in New York.

One-man shows: Egan Gallery, New York, 1948; Sidney Janis Gallery, New York, 1953, 1956; School of the Museum of Fine Arts, Boston, 1953; Workshop Art Center, Washington, D.C., 1953.

Included in: The New Decade, Whitney Museum of American Art, New York, shown thereafter in San Francisco, Los Angeles, Colorado Springs, and St Louis, 1955–6.

Group Exhibitions outside the United States of America: U.S. Representation, XXIV Biennale, Venice, 1948; U.S. Representation, XXV Biennale, Venice, 1950; U.S. Representation, I Bienal, São Paulo, 1951; *American Vanguard Art for Paris*, Galerie de France, Paris, 1952 (shown at Sidney Janis Gallery, New York, 1951–2); U.S. Representation, II Bienal, São Paulo, 1953; U.S. Representation, XXVII Biennale, Venice, 1954; *Modern Art in the United States: Selections from the Collections of The Museum of Modern Art, New York*, Paris, Zurich, Barcelona, Frankfurt, London, The Hague, Vienna, and Belgrade, 1955–6; U.S. Representation, XXVIII Biennale, Venice, 1956; U.S. Representation, 3rd International Contemporary Art Exhibition, India, six cities, 1957.

*40 *Painting* (1948)
Oil and ripolin enamel on canvas $42\frac{5}{8} \times 56\frac{1}{8}$ in.
Lent by The Museum of Modern Art, New York (Purchase)

*41 *Woman I* (1950–2)
Oil with charcoal on canvas $75\frac{7}{8} \times 58$ in.
Lent by The Museum of Modern Art, New York (Purchase)

42 *Woman II* (1952)
Oil on canvas 59×43 in.
Lent by The Museum of Modern Art, New York
(Gift of Mrs John D. Rockefeller III)

43 *Police Gazette* (1955)
Oil on canvas $43 \times 50\frac{1}{4}$ in.
Lent by Mr and Mrs Walter Bareiss, Greenwich, Connecticut

*44 *February* (1957)
Oil on canvas $79\frac{1}{2} \times 69$ in.
Lent by Dr and Mrs Edgar Berman, Baltimore, Maryland

ROBERT MOTHERWELL

Biography: Born 1915, Aberdeen, Washington. Lived in San Francisco, 1918–37. Stanford University, California, B.A., 1937. To New York, 1939. Attended Columbia University, 1940–1. Travelled in Europe 1935, 1937–9, 1955. First exhibited in International Surrealist Exhibition organized by Coordinating Council of the French Relief Societies, Whitelaw Reid Mansion, New York, 1942. In 1948, founder, with Baziotes, Newman, and Rothko, of school on East 8th Street, New York, 'Subjects of the Artist', out of which grew 'The Club' with weekly meetings of *avant-garde* artists. Co-editor of *Possibilities*, 1947–8; editor, *The Documents of Modern Art* series, 1944–51, and *Modern Artists in America*, No.1, New York, 1952. Painted mural for synagogue of Congregation B'nai Israel, Millburn, New Jersey, 1951. Visited West Germany under Exchange Program of Federal Republic of Germany, 1954. Teacher, Hunter College, New York, 1951 to present. Lives in New York.

One-man shows: Art of This Century (Peggy Guggenheim), New York, 1944; Kootz Gallery, New York, yearly 1946–53; Arts Club of Chicago, 1946; San Francisco Museum of Art, 1946; Galerie Jeanne Bucher, Paris, 1946; Oberlin College, Ohio, 1953; Sidney Janis Gallery, New York, 1957.

Included in: 14 Americans, The Museum of Modern Art, New York, 1946; *The New Decade*, Whitney Museum of American Art, New York, shown thereafter in San Francisco, Los Angeles, Colorado Springs, and St Louis, 1955–6.

Group Exhibitions outside the United States of America: Kootz Gallery Group, Galerie Maeght, Paris, 1947; U.S. Representation, II Bienal, São Paulo, 1951; *American Vanguard Art for Paris*, Galerie de France, Paris, 1952 (shown at Sidney Janis Gallery, New York, 1951–2); U.S. Representation, Tenth Inter-American Conference, Caracas, 1954; U.S. Representation, 3rd International Art Exhibition, Japan, eight cities, 1955; *Modern Art in the United States: Selections from the Collections of The Museum of Modern Art, New York*, Paris, Zurich, Barcelona, Frankfurt, London, The Hague, Vienna, and Belgrade, 1955–6.

★45 *Personage with Yellow Ochre and White* 1947
Oil on canvas 72 × 54 in.
Lent by The Museum of Modern Art, New York
(Gift of Mr and Mrs Samuel M. Kootz)

★46 *The Voyage* 1949
Oil and tempera on paper on composition board 48 × 94 in.
Lent by The Museum of Modern Art, New York
(Gift of Mrs John D. Rockefeller III)

★47 *Elegy for the Spanish Republic XXXV* 1954–8
Oil on canvas 80 × 100¼ in.
Lent by Mr and Mrs Albert Newman, Chicago

48 *Je t'aime, Number III, With Loaf of Bread* 1955
Oil on canvas 72 × 54 in.
Lent by Mr and Mrs Clement Greenberg, New York

49 *Jour la Maison, Nuit la Rue* 1957
Oil on canvas 70 × 90 in.
Lent by Sidney Janis Gallery, New York

BARNETT NEWMAN

Biography: Born 1905, New York. City College of New York, B.A., 1927; graduate work at Cornell University, Ithaca, New York. Studied at Art Students League, New York, 1922–6, with Duncan Smith, John Sloan, and William von Schlegel. In 1948, founder with Baziotes, Motherwell, and Rothko of school on East 8th Street, New York, 'Subjects of the Artist', out of which grew 'The Club' with weekly meetings of *avant-garde* artists. Lives in New York.

One-man shows: Betty Parsons Gallery, New York, 1950, 1951; Bennington College, Bennington, Vermont, 1958.

★50 *Abraham* 1949
Oil on canvas 84 × 35½ in.
Lent by Betty Parsons Gallery, New York

★51 *Concord* (1949)
Oil on canvas 90 × 54 in.
Lent by Mrs Betty Parsons, New York

52 *Horizon Light* 1949
Oil on canvas 30½ × 72½ in.
Lent by Mr and Mrs Thomas Sills, New York

★53 *Adam* 1951–2
Oil on canvas 95⅝ × 79⅝ in.
Lent by Mr and Mrs Ben Heller, New York

JACKSON POLLOCK

Biography: Born 1912, Cody, Wyoming; grew up in Arizona and California. Began study of painting at Manual Arts High School, Los Angeles, 1925–9. To New York, 1929; studied with Thomas Benton at Art Students' League, 1929–31. Trips to West in 1930, 1931, 1932, and 1934. Worked on WPA Federal Art Project, New York, 1938–42. Lived in Springs, Long Island, New York, from 1946 until his death in 1956.

One-man shows: Art of This Century (Peggy Guggenheim), New York, 1943 and yearly 1945–7; Arts Club of Chicago, 1945, 1951; San Francisco Museum of Art, 1945; Betty Parsons Gallery, New York, yearly 1948–51 (two exhibitions in 1949); Museo Correr, Venice, and Galleria d'Arte del Naviglio, Milan (both presented by Peggy Guggenheim), 1950; Studio Paul Facchetti, Paris (presented by Michel Tapié), 1952; Bennington College, Bennington, Vermont, 1952; Williams College, Williamstown, Massachusetts, 1952; Kunsthaus, Zurich, 1953; Sidney Janis Gallery, New York, 1952, 1954–5, 1957 (drawings only); The Museum of Modern Art, New York, 1956; U.S. Representation, IV Bienal, São Paulo, 1957.

Included in: 15 Americans. The Museum of Modern Art, New York, 1952; *The New Decade*, Whitney Museum of American Art, New York, shown thereafter in San Francisco, Los Angeles, Colorado Springs, and St Louis, 1955–6.

Group Exhibitions outside the United States of America: La Collezione Peggy Guggenheim, XXIV Biennale and Museo Internazionale d'Arte Moderna, Venice, 1948, shown thereafter in Florence and Milan, 1949, and Amsterdam, Brussels, and Zurich, 1951; U.S. Representation, XXV Biennale, Venice, 1950; U.S. Representation, I Bienal, São Paulo, 1951; U.S. Representation, 1st International Art Exhibition, Japan, five cities, 1952; U.S. Representation, 2nd International Contemporary Art Exhibition, India, five cities, 1953; *American Vanguard Art for Paris*, Galerie de France, Paris, 1952 (shown at Sidney Janis Gallery, New York, 1951–2); 12 *Modern American Painters and Sculptors*, Paris, Zurich, Düsseldorf, Stockholm, Helsinki, and Oslo. 1953–4; *Tendances Actuelles*, Kunsthalle, Berne, 1955; *Modern Art in the United States: Selections from the Collections of the Museum of Modern Art, New York*, Paris, Zurich, Barcelona, Frankfurt, London, The Hague, Vienna, and Belgrade, 1955–6; U.S. Representation, XXVIII Biennale, Venice, 1956; U.S. Representation, 3rd International Contemporary Art Exhibition, India, six cities, 1957; 75 *Paintings from the Solomon R. Guggenheim Museum, New York*, London, The Hague, Helsinki, Rome, Cologne, and Paris, 1957–8.

*54 *Number 8* (1949)
Oil and aluminium on canvas $34 \times 71\frac{1}{2}$ in.
Lent by Mr and Mrs Roy R. Neuberger, New York

55 *Number 26* (1951)
Oil on canvas $54\frac{1}{4} \times 36\frac{1}{2}$ in.
Lent by Sidney Janis Gallery, New York

*56 *Number 27* 1951
Duco on canvas $55\frac{3}{4} \times 75\frac{1}{4}$ in.
Lent by Sidney Janis Gallery, New York

*57 *Number 12* 1952
Oil on canvas $101\frac{7}{8} \times 89$ in.
Lent by Nelson A. Rockefeller, New York

MARK ROTHKO

Biography: Born 1903, Dvinsk, Russia. To U.S.A., 1913; grew up in Portland, Oregon. Attended Yale University, 1921–3. Began painting in 1926; studied at Art Students' League, New York, with Max Weber. Founding member, with Gottlieb, of 'The Ten' group, 1935. Worked on WPA Federal Art Project, New York, 1936–7. In 1948, founder with Baziotes, Motherwell, and Newman, of school on East 8th Street, New York, 'Subjects of the Artist', out of which grew 'The Club' with weekly meetings of *avant-garde* artists. Taught at California School of Fine Arts, San Franciso, summers 1947, 1949; Brooklyn College, New York, 1951–4. Lives in New York.

One-man shows: Portland (Oregon) Art Museum, 1933 (water-colours, drawings); Contemporary Arts, New York 1933; Art of This Century (Peggy Guggenheim), New York, 1945; Mortimer Brandt Gallery (Betty Parsons' contemporary section), New York, 1946 (water-colours); San Francisco Museum of Art, 1946; Santa Barbara Museum of Art, California, 1946; Betty Parsons Gallery, New York, yearly 1947–9, 1951; Rhode Island School of Design, Providence, 1954; Art Institute of Chicago, 1955; Sidney Janis Gallery, New York, 1955, 1958.

Included in: Group show (with Marcel Gromaire and Joseph Solman), Neumann-Willard Gallery, New York, 1940; 15 *Americans*. The Museum of Modern Art, New York, 1952.

Group Exhibitions outside the United States of America: U.S. Representation, Tenth Inter-American Conference Caracas, 1954; *Modern Art in the United States: Selections from the Collections of The Museum of Modern Art, New York*, Paris, Zurich, Barcelona, Frankfurt, London, The Hague, Vienna, and Belgrade, 1955–6; U.S. Representation, 3rd International Contemporary Art Exhibition, India, six cities, 1957.

*58 *Number 10* 1950
Oil on canvas $90\frac{3}{8} \times 57\frac{1}{8}$ in.
Lent by The Museum of Modern Art, New York (Gift of Philip C. Johnson)

59 *Number 7* 1951
Oil on canvas $94\frac{1}{2} \times 54\frac{3}{4}$ in.
Lent by Mrs Betty Parsons, New York

60 *Earth and Green* 1954–5
Oil on canvas $90\frac{3}{8} \times 73\frac{1}{2}$ in.
Lent by Mr and Mrs Ben Heller, New York

*61 *The Black and the White* 1956
Oil on canvas $94 \times 53\frac{3}{4}$ in.
Lent by Dr and Mrs Frank Stanton, New York

*62 *Tan and Black on Red* 1957
Oil on canvas $69\frac{3}{8} \times 53\frac{3}{8}$ in.
Lent by Mr and Mrs I. Donald Grossman, New York

THEODOROS STAMOS

Biography: Born 1922, New York. At 14, won scholarship to the American Artists' School, New York; studied sculpture with Simon Kennedy and Joseph Konzal, 1936–9. Painted in the West and British Columbia, 1947–8. Travelled in France, Italy, and Greece, 1948–9. Taught at Black Mountain College, North Carolina, 1950; Cummington School of Art, Massachusetts, 1952–3. Awarded Tiffany Fellowship, 1951. Lives in New York and East Marion, Long Island, New York.

One-man shows: Wakefield Gallery, New York, 1943; Mortimer Brandt Gallery (Betty Parsons' contemporary section), New York, 1944, 1946; Betty Parsons Gallery, New York, 1947, 1949, yearly 1951–3, 1956; Margaret Brown Gallery, Boston, 1948, 1950; Phillips Gallery, Washington, D.C., 1950, 1954; Baldwin Kingrey, Chicago, 1952; Philadelphia Art Alliance, 1957; Gump's, San Francisco, 1957; André Emmerich Gallery, New York, 1958.

Included in: The New Decade, Whitney Museum of American Art, New York, shown thereafter in San Francisco, Los Angeles, Colorado Springs, and St Louis, 1955–6.

Group Exhibitions outside the United States of America: U.S. Representation, 1st International Art Exhibition, Japan, five cities, 1952; U.S. Representation, *International Exhibition of Painters Under 35*, Rome, Brussels, Paris, 1955; U.S. Representation, 3rd International Art Exhibition, Japan, eight cities, 1955; *Modern Art in the United States: Selections from the Collections of The Museum of Modern Art, New York*, Paris, Zurich, Barcelona, Frankfurt, London, The Hague, Vienna, and Belgrade, 1955–6.

63 *Red Sea Terrace, Number 1* (1952)
Oil on canvas $92 \times 70\frac{1}{4}$ in.
Lent by André Emmerich Gallery, New York

64 *Heart of Willow – Sun* (1957)
Oil on canvas $79 \times 56\frac{1}{4}$ in.
Lent by André Emmerich Gallery, New York